Routledge Revivals

Measuring Quality: Education Indicators

Moves to develop indicators about school effectiveness and performance have been driven by national trends and debates about performance and accountability. Nationally set indicators – such as the standard assessment tasks, or the publication of performance in public examinations – have increasingly become part of the new education currency: a medium for exercising choice and decision-making in the new education market place. As contributors to this book suggest, such a framework is not unproblematic.

Originally published in 1994, this book offers a number of insights into the general debate about performance indicators at the time. It explores the background to the debate; the differing perspectives of policy-makers and practitioners; and the purpose, audiences and values of education indicators, both in the UK and elsewhere.

Measuring Quality
Education Indicators – United Kingdom and International Perspectives

Edited by
Kathryn Riley and Desmond Nuttall

First published in 1994
by The Falmer Press

This edition first published in 2018 by Routledge
2 Park Square, Milton Park, Abingdon, Oxon OX14 4RN

and by Routledge
711 Third Avenue, New York, NY 10017

Routledge is an imprint of the Taylor & Francis Group, an informa business

© 1994 K.A. Riley and D.L. Nuttall

The right of Kathryn Riley and Desmond Nuttall to be identified as editors of this work has been asserted by them in accordance with sections 77 and 78 of the Copyright, Designs and Patents Act 1988.

All rights reserved. No part of this book may be reprinted or reproduced or utilised in any form or by any electronic, mechanical, or other means, now known or hereafter invented, including photocopying and recording, or in any information storage or retrieval system, without permission in writing from the publishers.

Publisher's Note
The publisher has gone to great lengths to ensure the quality of this reprint but points out that some imperfections in the original copies may be apparent.

Disclaimer
The publisher has made every effort to trace copyright holders and welcomes correspondence from those they have been unable to contact.

A Library of Congress record exists under ISBN: 0750702605

ISBN: 978-1-138-30122-1 (hbk)
ISBN: 978-0-203-73266-3 (ebk)
ISBN: 978-1-138-30125-2 (pbk)

Measuring Quality:
Education Indicators — United Kingdom and International Perspectives

PROFESSOR DESMOND L. NUTTALL — A TRIBUTE

This book is dedicated to Desmond Nuttall who died in October 1993, at the age of 49.

Desmond was an outstanding educational researcher whose influence was international. His passion for education was evidenced in every appointment he undertook: the National Foundation for Educational Research; the Schools Council; Secretary to the Middlesex Regional Examination Board; Professor at the Open University; the Inner London Education Authority (where he was Director of Research and Statistics); the London School of Economics; and finally the Institute of Education where (to the delight of many), he was appointed Professor of Curriculum and Assessment Studies in 1992.

He was a man of great energy and enthusiasm with little sense of personal importance but a keen sense of the importance of ideas and of the potential influence of meticulously carried out research.

His openness led him to want to open doors for others, to give them opportunities to meet new people, or to think new ideas. He relished the skills and gifts of others, and nurtured his large circle of friends and colleagues in Britain and abroad.

He is a great lose to the world of education and to his friends and colleagues.

Kathryn Riley, December 1993

Measuring Quality:
Education Indicators — United Kingdom and International Perspectives

Edited by

Kathryn A. Riley and Desmond L. Nuttall

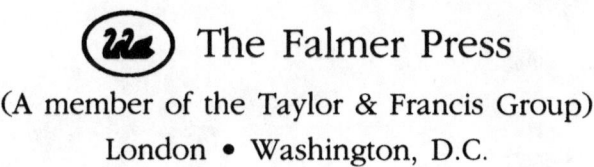 The Falmer Press

(A member of the Taylor & Francis Group)
London • Washington, D.C.

UK　　　The Falmer Press, 4 John Street, London WC1N 2ET
USA　　The Falmer Press, Taylor & Francis Inc., 1900 Frost Road, Suite 101, Bristol, PA 19007

© K.A. Riley and D.L. Nuttall 1994

All rights reserved. No part of this publication may be reproduced, stored in a retrieval system, or transmitted in any form or by any means, electronic, mechanical, photocopying, recording or otherwise, without permission in writing from the Publisher.

First published in 1994

A catalogue record for this book is available from the British Library

Library of Congress Cataloging-in-Publication Data are available on request

ISBN 0 7507 0260 5 cased
ISBN 0 7507 0261 3 paper

Jacket design by Caroline Archer

Typeset in 11/13 pt Garamond by
Graphicraft Typesetters Ltd., Hong Kong

Contents

A Tribute ii

Chapter 1
The Framework 1
Kathryn A. Riley and Desmond L. Nuttall

Chapter 2
Education Indicators: Officials, Ministers and the Demand
for Information 6
Alan Ruby

Chapter 3
Choosing Indicators 17
Desmond L. Nuttall

Chapter 4
How Indicators Have Been Used in the USA 41
Ramsay Selden

Chapter 5
Quality, Surveillance and Performance Measurement ... 49
Kieron Walsh

Chapter 6
Performance Indicators: Flourish or Perish? 69
John Gray and Brian Wilcox

Chapter 7
Following the Education Indicators Trail in the Pursuit
of Quality 87
Kathryn A. Riley

Measuring Quality

Chapter 8
A Role for Parents, Students and Teachers in School
Self-Evaluation and Development Planning   100
John MacBeath

Chapter 9
Measuring Performance — National Contexts and Local
Realities   122
Kathryn A. Riley and Desmond L. Nuttall

Notes on Contributors   133

Index   135

Chapter 1

The Framework

Kathryn A. Riley and Desmond L. Nuttall

Overview

Moves to develop indicators about school effectiveness and performance have been driven by national trends and by a broader debate about performance and accountability[1]. Nationally set indicators of performance — such as the standard assessment tasks, or the publication of performance on public examination — have increasingly become part of the new education currency: a medium for exercising choice and decision-making in the new education market place. As contributors to the book will suggest, such a framework is not unproblematic.

This book offers some insights into the general debate about education, or performance indicators. It explores the background to the debate; the differing perspectives of policy-makers and practitioners; and the purposes, audiences and values of education indicators, both in the UK and international context. It builds on an international symposium on education indicators, held in 1991, which brought together a wide-range of participants to evaluate progress in the field of education indicators[2].

Contributors to the book do not argue that education indicators offer a panacea to educational ills. But readers are offered an understanding of the issues involved; an appreciation of the role of indicators in evaluation and in sustaining school improvement; and a critique of their limitations. The contributors focus on both the context for measuring performance and the application of performance indicators at national and local systems levels, and at school level. The authors provide an overview of the current issues in performance measurement and illuminate the interrelated but different roles played by politicians, policy-makers and practitioners in the development, interpretation and use of education indicators.

Contributions to the book focus on four major themes: why policy-makers require information about performance; how such information relates to national contexts; the limitations of performance measurement; and the challenges in applying such information at the local system level.

Providing Information to Meet the Needs of Policy-makers

Alan Ruby (chapter 2) suggests that education data collected in the past has been relatively simplistic and based on attempts to measure the size of the education system and its 'throughput'. From his perspective as a senior education adviser to the Australian Government, he suggests that politicians today — both in Australia and other OECD countries — increasingly require information about outcomes and in a timescale which is attuned to political realities. Such demands have implications for education officials who need to strengthen their skills in interpreting data; become more involved in specific policy-making problems; and give greater attention to data systems.

Desmond Nuttall (chapter 3) draws on work from a major OECD project on education indicators to examine the purposes and definitions of indicators and the lessons to be learned from past attempts to develop indicator systems. He explores the factors which have influenced the selection of particular indicators and suggests that research knowledge, technical, practical and policy considerations, as well as who the choosers are, influence the development of an indicator system.

Education Systems and National Contexts

Questions that are central to the concerns of politicians reflect different national contexts and purposes as Ruby suggests in his chapter. Ramsay Selden (chapter 4) describes the context for introducing a national indicators system in the USA. He traces the origins of the initiative's development and suggests that the initiative emerged from growing national concerns about the poor level of pupil performance and a belief that Federal Government should take a more defined role in setting national goals and in making state by state comparisons about performance. He draws on activities within the different states to illustrate how indicators can be used for very different sorts of purposes. In South Carolina, for example, performance indicators (as part of a wider model of accountability) have resulted in monetary rewards for good performance and sanctions, such as the removal of administrators, for poor performance.

The Limitations of Performance Measurement Systems

Selden also highlights the weaknesses in linking performance to pay and suggests that such systems can end up not necessarily rewarding the successful. He argues that whilst the introduction of performance indicators provides a useful focus on achievement, top-down approaches aimed at using testing to bring about change are limited, particularly when such developments are not linked to any concurrent efforts to provide support for school improvement. He points out, for example, that initial findings from the state by state analysis of pupil performance in mathematics suggest that student performance is closely associated with the levels of mathematics to which teachers were taught at colleges and their recent in-service professional development.

Kieron Walsh (chapter 5) also raises questions about linking performance to pay. He analyzes the broader issues around the rise of performance measurement within the public sector and argues that recent developments have ignored the complexities and difficulties of developing effective systems. Measuring performance does not automatically improve performance. Measurements need to be introduced for a system and not just for individuals, or individual organizations within that system. Otherwise hospitals, for example, might increase their 'efficiency' by discharging patients more rapidly — a move that would have a significant impact on housing and social services.

Walsh goes on to explore the problems associated with what he describes as a *surveillance-based* approach to performance measurement: an approach which he suggests can leads to rigidity, inflexibility and reduced learning. If organizations are to grow, he argues, they must be able to learn from their own mistakes. Problems are not necessarily resolved by tightening up inspection procedures, or introducing more indicators but by improving management systems and staff training and support.

Applying Indicators at the Local Systems Level

John Gray and Brian Wilcox (chapter 6) draw on a major survey of inspectors and advisers to establish what quantitative measures local education authorities have used to develop their framework for measuring performance. They examine the stumbling blocks in establishing indicators and suggest that if effective performance indicators are to be developed which will support the improvement of quality, then practitioners and policy-makers need to be clear about what counts as performance indicators; formulate a wide range of measures; and develop indicators which look at education processes, as well those which look at outcomes.

Kathryn Riley (chapter 7) charts the strategies and processes which local education authorities and schools have adopted in developing education indicators. She argues that indicators can be used to enhance decision-making and widen accountability — if LEAs are clear about their purposes. Education indicators also need to be integrated into a wider evaluative system which draws together inspection and self-evaluation.

Riley concludes that the task of linking the development of education indicators to improvements in the quality of the education service is likely to be made more difficult in the future by the requirements of the 1992 Education Schools Act (which has severed inspection from advice, support and development of schools) and by the 1993 Education Act (which has diminished the capacity of the local education authority to develop a quality framework and to support school improvement).

The chapter by Riley also illustrates the difficulties created by the increasing gap between the objectives and requirements of central government and the activities of local authorities. The Scottish context for change is, however, markedly different as John MacBeath illustrates in chapter 8.

MacBeath describes how the Scottish Office Education Department has worked to develop a a national indicators system which fosters ownership amongst Scottish regional education authorities and schools. He outlines how this partnership has taken place through a collaborative project with school administrators, classroom teachers, parents and pupils which compares perceptions about school performance. The major objective of the project has been to enhance school improvement: a theme that is explored in some detail in the concluding chapter by Riley and Nuttall.

Notes

1 This issue is discussed more fully in the concluding chapter.
2 The conference (which was organized by Kathryn Riley and Desmond Nuttall) was held at the Institute of Local Government Studies, University

of Birmingham, 1–2 July 1991. Conference contributors included a number of contributors to this book: Desmond Nuttall, Kathryn Riley, Alan Ruby and Ramsay Selden and also Norbetto Bottani and Isabelle Delfau from the OECD (Co-directors of the International Education Indicators Project — INES).

Chapter 2

Education Indicators: Officials, Ministers and the Demand for Information

Alan Ruby

Politicians in all Western countries increasingly demand information that is simple, comparable, timely and which can be translated into the public arena. This chapter sketches out the implications and challenges of such demands for policy-makers.

Education officials in most Western countries have spent most of the last ten years being devolved, reformed, restructured, down sized and outplaced. Schools have become, or been exhorted to become, more self-managing, more client oriented, more outcome oriented and more accountable. As a consequence of these changes there has been and continues to be increasing demands on political decision-makers for information.

In the Anglo-Saxon countries the relationship between officials and 'ministers' is often summarized as 'advise, counsel and warn': to advise about the best ways to do things, to counsel the Minister about his/her responsibilities and to caution them against the inappropriate, the foolhardy and the counterproductive. We give facts, offer opinions and display our values. The essence of our business is information.

As information specialists our first response to these demands for information was literal compliance. We gave our Ministers *more*. We increased the quantity assuming the issue was volume not quality or timelines or 'relevance'. This failed — in most cases, or at least produced confusion.

The second response was didactic. Let me illustrate. In the early 1980s I was asked by my then Minister to provide the pupil teacher ratios (PTR) for ten specific countries. With the naivety of a junior official I replied: 'I'm not sure that you actually want that information. Its not really what you need to answer the question I assume you're grappling with.' Ignoring the silence I continued: 'PTR is not a good measure of relative resource allocation or usage. It does not necessarily translate into relative instructional time or offer valid proxies for inputs into the specific process of learning. PTR also ignores the fact that there are a lot of adults in schools who make substantial contributions to learning, both direct and indirect, who are not teachers.' I enumerated many categories and offered the observation that an adult to pupil ratio might be more meaningful if the data were available.

I went on to discuss technical difficulties in the comparable definition of 'teacher' across the ten countries, the differences between the ten countries and Australia which further limited the usefulness of the data and ended up with a survey of the data problems in this area both nationally and internationally. He with what I now see as inestimable patience thanked me and said 'Now, give me the data.' I did.

Reflecting on this exchange I was led to one conclusion — I could not deny the legitimacy of his request. I was unable to do so, and still am unable, not just because of notions of democracy and good government but also because we do not know how ministers actually make decisions. Personal and political decisions are so complex that we are unable to isolate and comprehend how all the different elements and factors are balanced and interconnected. In this context we cannot deny a decision-maker information sought because we believe it inappropriate to the task we assume is at hand. So the didactic response was also a 'failure' although it did strengthen our understandings about the weaknesses of our data. This has caused us to try to improve the quality of our information. To do that we need to understand then what has produced the demand for better information.

Education Reform and the Demand for Information

Apart from curiosity the four conventional motivations for wanting information are: the pragmatic, the moral, the conservative and the rational (Mitchell, 1989).

The pragmatic is, well, does it work? The moral: is it good? The conservative, which is not politically conservative in the sense of party political: is it necessary and the rational; can we make it better?

Those simple, conventional motivations do dominate public life but they do not help us understand why we have suddenly been faced, as officials, with demands for better information. If you stand back from the reforms of the last ten years around the world, the reforms in education and training, we can start to discern some other demands for information and some other motivations or rationales. The first one is that politicians in most OECD countries demand information that will guide and monitor their reforms. Politicians increasingly want to know if their reforms are working.

This reflects a pragmatic interest in effectiveness and good management that has influenced politics in Western nations. It also illustrates an increased interest in immediate benefits, not just for electoral advantage, but as a product of a greater emphasis on 'outcomes'.

Structural reforms particularly those involving shifts in responsibility such as the devolution of decision making power to schools, as in many Australian States, and the centralization of curriculum in the UK, or those that involve the allocation of additional funds for particular practices or behaviours such as teacher tests (Texas) or career ladders (Tennessee under Governor Alexander) are linked with demands for better or more information. Governments or ministers seem concerned that having mandated some reform they then need to monitor the process as well as looking for an outcome. They need and look for different forms of information produced by different mechanisms so they can maintain political accountability.

Accountability reforms which have also been popular in the last ten years also produce — indeed they are usually based on — demands for more or different information. Sometimes it is a single instrument while at others it is a whole process of evaluation, improvement and measurement such as school improvement strategies.

Accountability takes on greater significance when social expenditure is contracting or under scrutiny because of a general contraction in public expenditure. It becomes much more important that expenditure is both efficient and effective. To demonstrate this more or better information is required.

Rational models of decision making which have also become more influential in the last ten-fifteen years reinforce this trend. Management by objectives, program budgeting and the like all depend on explicit goal setting and documentation generating more information and a demand for existing information to be transformed into new reporting frameworks.

Better information to promote and defend ideological commitments is another powerful political motivation. There are many sorts of commitments which generate requests for information. Policies which focus on the individual choice of schools and competition between schools require information to guide and stimulate choice and compare school performance. Similarly policies which include the differential allocation of resources can be buttressed by information about relative success between class or racial groups. A ready example is the additional resources supplied for schools serving concentrations of Aborigines whose participation in Australian schooling is four times less than the average.

Gaining the resources necessary for differential assistance and getting the 'right' quantum requires information about relative success for particular population groups. It generates a demand for information to be disaggregated and presented in a way which informs debate about priorities.

These themes and others are readily discernible in the policies of governments of all persuasions across the OECD countries. How will they influence individual ministers and affect how officials go about discharging their responsibilities? Perhaps we should answer this by pursuing the issue from the perspective of a Minister.

What Do They Want?

The characteristics of 'good' information in the eyes of policy makers is information that is *simple, comparable and timely*. These are the hallmarks sought by all data managers and policy analysts. The emphasis politicians place on them relates to a desire to be in control of the information at hand and a disjunction in how these three words are interpreted. The politician is seeking simplicity to order or reduce the complexity confronting him or her and comparability to trade off or exclude some options and timeliness to deal with the seemingly ever shortening timescales confronting governments. Officials, and particularly those producing statistics, give quite different weights and nuances to these terms. Some tend to describe comparability in technical terms, emphasizing such things as common definitions and collection times.

In addition to these qualities politicians want information which is *accessible, direct and public*. These three qualities describe information which is easy to interpret, relates closely and obviously to the phenomenon or policy question at hand, and is in the public domain or at least readily understood by the public when it is released. These qualities have shaped public reporting strategies in many countries. In the USA these have included the infamous wallchart displaying a disparate range of measures comparing the fifty states and the more balanced Conditions of Education Report. In Australia the Annual National Report on Schooling and its statistical annex are distributed to all schools in the country and to the parent groups.

The emphasis on these qualities can have some questionable side effects. One example, in the United Kingdom, is the debate about the relative interests of reporting raw scores or those adjusted to show 'value added'. Some have reduced the issue to the notion that adjusting for differences in say socioeconomic background or ability of intakes is 'cooking the data' so that it is incomprehensible to parents who need to make an informed choice between schools.

Without dismissing either the pros or cons of the debate about value added measures, it is more important for the analysis to ask if these characteristics describe our existing information. If so, how well does it fit with the demands of policy-makers?

What is Wrong With What We Have Now

Education officials in all Western countries collect data, lots of data, especially data on inputs. How many students, how many teachers, how many classrooms? It is data addressing the concerns and policy goals of a time when Governments were establishing school systems and promoting the common school as the lot, if not the right, of all young people. In simplistic terms it is data measuring the size of the system and its *'throughput'*.

There was little demand or need for data on the working of the system because in most instances it was highly regulated with central prescription of curricula either directly or through examination bodies. In some countries the inspectorial tradition fostered compliance. In the USA the picture is more complex with the common school being a metaphor for the melting pot philosophy of an emerging nation and control and compliance being tied to local political structures.

Choice which has been such a stimulus to demands for information was not an issue because there was, by definition, no difference between schools and hence no reason to choose. Even worse, choice promoted inefficiencies because it left places empty and created excess demand in popular schools. This was clearly unsatisfactory when the first call on capital funds was the creation of new places for those who were not receiving schooling. It is only now in times of excess supply of school places that choice can act as a tool to promote efficiency.

There are big gaps in these large data sets. There is very little on outcomes, on student achievement. What there is tends to be at the wrong level, difficult to aggregate and not comparable across schools, race or class groups or different providers — states, local authorities or districts.

There are other shortcomings in current data sets. The criteria adopted by the OECD/CERI international indicators project for high quality measures of education systems set benchmarks for indicators which few existing education statistical collections meet. Three of these criteria are particularly relevant to this discussion:

- indicators should measure ubiquitous features of schooling — things that can be found in some forum throughout the system — so that comparisons can be made across diverse contexts;
- indicators should measure enduring features of the school system so that trends can be analyzed over time;
- indicators should be readily understood by broad audiences. (based on Oakes, 1986).

How Should 'We' Respond?

The premise for any response must be that the demand for better information is legitimate and should be fulfilled within the bounds of feasibility and available resources. But the response cannot just be a technical one of creating and passing on this 'better' information. We must strengthen our analytical capacities to ensure we continue to be effective advisers. As counsellors we have an obligation to interpret the information and relate it to the issues at hand. We must also guard against the provision of misinformation and limit the opportunities for and correct, as far as possible, misinterpretation. In short we must adhere to our traditional responsibilities knowing that our task is harder than before.

In addition we must strive to improve the validity of information and the ways in which it is used. One step is to broaden the coverage of data systems to encompass the whole of the education process. This requires an underpinning conceptual model of the process. This need not be elaborate to gain some benefit. For example, the simple four part model used in the beginning of INES: *Context, Input, Process* and *Output* was very useful. It drew attention to the gaps in the array of indicators and the need for coherence in the final set.

It is not just a matter of enlarging the data set. This is neither feasible nor desirable. There needs to be some systematic selection of what new elements will be created and some thoughtful consideration of whose interests should be served by the provision of better information about particular aspects of education.

How Do You Create Better Information?

The questions of 'what to include', 'what to omit' and 'why' swirl around all attempts to create better information. The swirl of contending issues and audiences and the competing rationales is usually brought to order by fiscal constraints: how much will it cost. This discipline does not necessarily produce better information.

The notion of *relevance* offers another avenue for resolving the competition. This requires the capacity and willingness to guard against topicality and propinquity and differentiate between enduring values and the ephemeral slogans of political life.

Relevance is sometimes used to justify data collections to address immediate concerns and problems as 'particular events'. This tends to limit the generalizability of the data to other contexts or other phenomena which are expressions of the same policy question. The challenge is to relate the topical to recurring questions or issues. *Propinquity* is harder to resist. Collecting data just because it happens to be there or handy or might be relevant is a temptation for all of us. The by-products are more complex databases and static, noise in information systems caused by monitoring variables which do not have strategic value for policy makers. The hallmarks of relevance are similar to the quality benchmarks set in the INES project: data which has some direct connection with the issue at hand and to other expressions of the same policy problem; data which describes or relates to an enduring feature of education systems; data monitoring phenomenon which are subject to influence — what we usually call malleable variables.

It is not an easy task to get agreement about enduring values and if and how they should be monitored. The importance of school attendance is a ready example. In the first phase of the INES project a colleague and I tried to convince our international collaborators that regular school attendance was an educational and social value of significance to all countries. There was reluctant agreement that there were educational benefits from children going to school every day and we pressed ahead with an attempt to get internationally comparable data on absenteeism. Table 2.1 shows the responses of some countries.

The range of responses reflects the different governance structures and policy orientations in the various countries (see Ruby, 1990, for a fuller discussion). The importance here is to show the difficulty of operationalizing even simple values.

Dealing with the *ephemeral* is not much easier. The half-life of political slogans is difficult to estimate. It is of course the time it takes for a catchphrase to go from an organizing point in all policy discussions

Table 2.1: Some countries responses to a proposed indicator of absenteeism

Belgium
'Information is only available at the school level ...'
'... (not attending school) ... is forbidden by law, but is uncontrolled ...'

Canada
'Not a priority in the perspective of international comparisons. However, the formal duration of the school year, as well as the extent of the weekly schedule remain valid process indicators.'

Japan
'... Our government does not have almost any political interest in the attendance rate.'

Netherlands
'... there is some information but the quality differs between municipalities ...'
'The attention is mainly given to long-term absenteeism ... (this) is directed to monitoring problem-pupils potential dropouts.'
'Research discovered that 15–20 per cent of all lessons in secondary education are not given because of sickness (teacher), examinations or staff meetings. This seems to be a far more serious problem than the absenteeism of pupils.'

Switzerland
'Absenteeism is no issue ... neither public opinion nor the educational administrators are concerned about absenteeism, and it is totally missing from public or administrative debate.'
'If it exists, then only on a marginal basis.'

USA
'Our data vary considerably from state to state, so we have difficulty producing good national estimates.'

West Germany
'The attendance rates for these grades (compulsory years) only depends on illness. Otherwise it would be 100 per cent. Therefore ... (attendance rates) ... don't apply.'

---

to a cliche. This time is influenced by such things as the power of the originator, changes in ministers and governments, novelty and scope of the slogan. Some persist for a long time and shape data systems. The French Government's commitment to a 'classroom a day' in the 1960s influenced its physical facilities data base. Others disappear without trace. The tests of relevance help to identify those slogans with long half-lives.

Another dimension to this debate about what to include or omit is the question of audience and purpose. Do politicians and the public want the same information for the same reasons? The tension for officials is to serve their Minister and acknowledge a wider responsibility to the public. The debate about 'whistleblowers', officials who release information about contentious government decisions, diverts attention from the real question: how an official can properly discharge that wider responsibility.

Measuring Quality

Freedom of information legislation which ensures access to all information, other than that relating to other individuals and advice to the executive, applies to the federal and most state government officials in Australia. We are also subject to public scrutiny before Committees of Parliaments, through the public release of audit and evaluation reports and by the Ombudsman and the Administrative Appeals Tribunal. In addition specialist advisory councils for Aborigines, people with disabilities and agencies with responsibilities for women and migrants are able to command the provision of data and information. In this context, assuming availability, an official tends to provide information on request.

Purpose is more difficult. The traditional debate in education about reporting on student achievement is summarized as 'teaching to the test'. The argument being that because assessment is always a selection from what was or should have been taught, teachers reduce what they teach to the tested, or testable, items. The outcome is a narrowing of the curriculum. Is this good or bad? Is it a distortion of priorities or a focussing of effort? This problem is not confined to student achievement testing but covers all policy domains where changes in data or scores produces a 'high stakes outcome'. Paying a 'bounty' for children with disabilities who are integrated into regular schools increases the number of children with disabilities identified in those schools without necessarily adding to the actual number of students.

One response to multiple audiences and ambiguity of purpose is to collect more. This tendency compounds the problem of existing data systems which suffer from over-inclusiveness. Again the most effective selection frame is to test the claims for new data against some criteria.

Stern and Hall (1987) working on the Conditions of Education publication in the USA emphasized the following points:

- Is it about a significant aspect of the education system?
- Can it be presented as a single valued statistic, or a composite index?
- Will it provide a benchmark for measuring change over time, or differences across geographic areas or institutions at a point in time?
- Does it represent a policy issue, or an aspect of education that might be altered by policy decision?
- Can it be readily understood?
- Will the data be reliable and not subject to significant modification as a result of response error, or changes in the personnel generating it?

How Should Officials React?

Technical responses to the demand for information, while important and badly needed, are not sufficient. Officials also need to improve their practice. They have to improve the ways they use information. *The first task* is to strengthen skills in interpreting and presenting data to promote better decision making. This includes identifying and communicating the constraints on the use of particular sets of information in specific circumstances. It also includes assessing the strength and reliability of data so that the inferences that might be drawn are sustainable.

The second task is to become more involved with the specification of policy problems, to get a better understanding of what data is needed and of the contexts in which they will be applied. Some see this as a threat to the traditional political neutrality of officials. It can be, if the official becomes partisan and offers information and advice which support only one view of the problem.

The third task is for senior officials to pay greater attention to monitoring and data systems, to ensure they retain currency and are used to address emerging policy problems. Too often senior officials are unaware of the data that is available which notwithstanding its limitations, could inform policy problems. Using systems frequently improves understanding of their strengths and weaknesses and enhances the capacity to use them creatively to inform policy questions.

The three tasks require officials to become better users of information which requires an investment of time in deepening understanding of the explanatory power of information. This also requires an understanding of how data is collected, of the definitions used, of when and how it was collected and for what purpose. A recent example from the Canberra Health System illustrates the importance of definitions. A dispute about a shortage of hospital beds revealed that the key indicator used by the health systems administrators was 'bed capacity'. This was defined to include beds, chairs and trolleys of which there were 910, 820 in operation. The doctors and nurses taking a simpler view of the world could only find 750 'beds'. Defending the difference the Minister pointed out that 'bed capacity' was calculated 'in accordance' with the National Minimum Data Set and that was the 'end of the story'. It was not a popular defence.

Conclusion

The demands for information have assailed education officials over the last ten years. In that time we have responded literally and provided more, producing confusion. Faced with confusion we tried to explain why more information was not required and found our advice unwelcome and unheeded. A third response is needed. It has to be a response based on a thoughtful analysis of the problem and of how it should be met. There are lessons to be learnt from the work of the OECD/CERI indicators project. The most powerful lesson is that demands for data should be analyzed using a framework which assesses the enduring value of the data sought. Finally, officials need to improve their practice as users of data to become better advisers.

References

MITCHELL, D.E. (1989) 'Measuring up: Standards for evaluating school reform' in SERGIOVANNI, T.J. and MOORE, J.H. (Eds) *Schooling for Tomorrow, Directing Reform To Issues that Count*, Sydney, Allyn and Bacon.

OAKES, J. (1986) *Education Indicators: A Guide for Policy Makers*, Centre for Policy Research in Education, October.

RUBY, A. (1990) 'Do common values produce common indicators?' in WYATT T. and RUBY, A. (Eds) *Education Indicators for Quality, Accountability and Better Practice,* Sydney, Conference of Directors of Education, Sydney.

STERN, J.D. and HALL, G. (1987) *Education Development at the Federal Level.* CES, OERI, USA Department of Education, April.

Chapter 3

Choosing Indicators

Desmond L. Nuttall

The aim of this chapter is to examine the factors that influence the selection of particular indicators as components of an indicator system, and to derive a general set of principles that would make the selection process more systematic. The chapter therefore starts with a clarification of the term 'indicator', and then considers what may be learnt from the history of indicator systems in other fields. In the light of this analysis, the chapter looks at the major considerations that govern the selection process and at how they have been embodied in lists of criteria proposed by workers in the field, before proposing such a set for use with educational indicators.

What are Indicators?

There is general consensus that indicators are designed to provide information about the state of an educational (or, more generally, a social) system. They act as an early-warning system that something may be going wrong, in the same way that the instruments on the dashboard of a car can alert the driver to a problem or reassure him or her that everything is functioning smoothly. A dial pointer moving into the red zone is only a symptom of some malfunction and further investigation is needed to establish the cause. Viewed as reassuring or warning devices, indicators conform to the dictionary definition; for example, the Oxford dictionary defines an indicator as 'that which points out or directs attention to something' (quoted by Johnstone, 1981, p. 2). If something is wrong, the indicators themselves do not provide the diagnosis or prescribe the remedy; they are simply suggestive of the need for action.

The consensus over the broad purpose of indicators does not extend to the precise definition of what an indicator is. Some reserve the definition to a narrowly quantitative one; thus,

Measuring Quality

> A third feature of an indicator is that it is something which is quantifiable. It is not a statement describing the state of a system. Instead it must be a real number to be interpreted according to the rules governing its formation. (*ibid*, p. 4)

Others take a much wider view, and would include descriptive or even evaluative statements within the scope of indicators (for example, Chartered Institute of Public Finance and Accountancy (CIPFA), 1988). Almost always, though, even the widest definition limits the concept to information, and excludes analysis or discussion.

The fears of those who adopt a wider view are that the limiting of the concept to just the quantitative will mean that indicators cannot portray the full richness and diversity of the educational process, and that, at worst, they will indicate merely the trivial and focus attention on the unimportant. This is similar to one of the major criticisms of quantitative research in education and the social sciences by those who espouse the qualitative approach, and as such goes beyond the scope of this chapter. Nevertheless, it is incumbent on those who propose indicators to demonstrate that they are not too reductionist, and will not divert attention from equally important (or even more important) goals.

It would seem that the more common view of indicators is of the quantitative variety. For example, in the survey carried out under the OECD Institutional Management in Higher Education programme, an indicator is defined as 'a numerical value . . .' and the OECD Indicators Project has tacitly taken the same view. The line between management statistics and indicators is not easily drawn, however. Some suggest that indicators imply a comparison against a reference point (as in a time series or an average), while by implication statistics do not, but in fact it is rare that the interpretation of even descriptive statistics dispenses with comparison. Others limit the term to composite statistics such as a student-teacher ratio, so that the number of students enrolled in a particular phase of education would not be considered an indicator (though it could well be an important item of management information).

A somewhat broader definition was adopted by Shavelson *et al* (1987): 'An indicator is an individual or a composite statistic that relates to a basic construct in education and is useful in a policy context' (p. 5). They deny that all statistics are indicators, though: 'Statistics qualify as indicators only if they serve as yardsticks (of the quality of education)' (*ibid*, p. 5).

The confusion over definition was noted by Jaeger (1978), who proposed that:

all variables that (1) represent the aggregate status or change in status of any group of persons, objects, institutions, or elements under study, and that (2) are essential to a report of status or change of status of the entities under study or to an understanding of the condition of the entities under study, should be termed indicators. I would not require that reports of status or change in status be in quantitative form, for narrative is often a better aid to comprehension and understanding of phenomena than is a numeric report. (pp. 285–7)

It therefore seems that there is no clear agreement on exactly what an indicator is or is not; Selden (1991) cuts the Gordian knot by proposing that we should drop preconceptions about what 'indicators' are and recognize that it is their *use* that makes them 'indicators'. For the purposes of this chapter, an indicator is taken to be *quantitative*, recognizing that it could stretch to a quantification of a professional subjective judgment (as in the rating of the quality of teaching); an indicator would *also be quoted alongside other similar indicators to allow comparison* (usually over time, but also with an average or norm, or with values from other institutions, regions or nations). Above all, indicators are seen *as part of a set or system of indicators* that together provide information designed to be greater than the sum of its parts, rather than something displayed in isolation (as test scores have been in some international comparisons of achievement in the past). This idea of an indicator system is discussed further below.

Indicators in the Policy-making Process

If there is no agreement on the definition of indicators, there is a large measure of agreement over their purpose, namely that they are designed to give information to policy-makers about the state of the educational system, either to demonstrate its accountability or, more commonly, to help in policy analysis, policy evaluation and policy formulation. The policy-makers can be at the national, regional or district level, within the institution itself (as senior managers or faculty managers), or even at a classroom level, where, in effect, the teacher is always reacting to information about the pupils' progress to adjust the pacing or focus of his/her teaching.

Indicators will naturally be only one of the aids in policy analysis, alongside such techniques as cost-benefit analysis and futures research, but nevertheless they are seen as an increasingly important contribution to *rational* policy analysis (Carley, 1980; Hogwood and Gunn, 1984). Moreover, indicators tend to send signals about what is or should be important, and thus contribute to the public identification of policy issues and concerns — the stream of public problems seen as important, as Kingdon (1984) put it. Indeed, Innes (1990) argued that 'social indicators ultimately have their most important role to play in framing the terms of policy discourse' (p. 431). She proposed an interpretative or phenomenological view of knowledge to help the recognition and comprehension of the badly needed integration of indicator concepts with the understandings of the public.

Others also take the view that research knowledge is not used directly by the policy-maker. Partly this is because there are limits to the rationality of the policy-making process, as argued by Cohen and Spillane, and partly because knowledge is only one of the influences upon policy-making, which is inevitably a political process (McDonnell, 1989). Indeed, the only function of knowledge in the policy-making process may be to alter the general climate of opinion (Nisbet and Broadfoot, 1980) or the *Zeitgeist.* Weiss (1979) sees its function as general 'enlightenment':

> Here it is not the findings of a single study nor even of related studies that directly affect policy. Rather it is the concepts and theoretical perspectives that social science research has engendered that permeate the policymaking process. (Weiss, 1979, p. 429, cited by McDonnell, 1989, p. 244)

The history in the USA of social indicators (which came to prominence in the 1960s and 1970s but faded away in the 1980s) shows that several factors contributed to their decline (analyzed in detail by Rockwell (1989) and in a symposium published in the *Journal of Public Policy* [Rose, 1990]).

The first factor was essentially political. Any indicator system embodies value judgments about what is meant by quality or desirable outcomes in education, nor is any underlying model or framework objective. The review by van Herpen (1989) demonstrates that such frameworks or models almost always have a bias towards one particular epistemological perspective of the education system (for example, the economic or the sociological). The meaning of the indicators (and their changes over time) thus becomes contentious, and there is a 'tendency for indicators to become vindicators' (Bulmer, 1990, p. 410) and for the reports to be 'rather bland compromises, deliberately presented without text that might link the data to policy' (Innes, 1990, p. 430).

Secondly, the system became divorced from the policy context and too theoretical and abstruse, run essentially for and by the social scientific community. Innes (1990) suggested that the social scientists had an overly simplistic and overly optimistic view of how and in what circumstances knowledge is used in the process of policy analysis, and of how straightforward it would be to develop indicators:

> They focussed energy on the measurement task, often to the exclusion of the political and institutional one. They did not recognize how the political and institutional issues would interact with decisions about methodology. (p. 431)

Bulmer (1990), attributed the lack of success of the social indicator movement to the failure of social science to become institutionalized in the governments of industrial societies, something that is particularly difficult to achieve under conservative administrations. MacRae (1985) concurred, suggesting a need for a 'technical community':

> an expert group that conducts and monitors research, but directs its work at concerns of citizens and public officials, not merely at improving its own theories (in the manner of a 'scientific community'). (p. 437)

Such groups have become more common in the last few years as policy analysts or researchers in the direct employ of national or local government.

The third and, according to Bulmer (1990), the most important factor lying behind relative failure of social indicators was the lack of general social scientific theories of a specificity that allowed the development of indicators to measure the theoretical constructs. Economic theories have been worked out in much more detail, and economic indicators have the advantage of a common measure of value (i.e. money), though they will sometimes include other kinds of numbers (for example, the unemployment rate). Notwithstanding the largely common measure, there are rival economic theories and much contention over the interpretation and explanation of indicators that spills into the media. But in other social sciences, Bulmer (1990) considered

Measuring Quality

that 'the absence of theory does not preclude the construction of indicators, but it means that when this happens, they often lack a clear rationale and conceptual justification' (p. 409).

How are Indicators Chosen?

There is clearly much to be learnt from the recent past about the factors that ought to be taken into consideration in creating an indicator system in education. There appear to be three basic sources of influence that interact in the creation of indicators: policy considerations, scientific/technical considerations, and practical ones. These are considered in turn in this section.

Policy Considerations

In the case of a general interest about the state of the educational system, some principle will govern the choice of indicators, but it may be as simple as the use of information already available. This seems to have been the case with the Wallchart in the USA, where only data that were routinely collected (for a variety of different purposes) were displayed in the Wallchart; they were chosen for their perceived relevance to appraise the educational performance of the fifty states. Some of the indicators in the Wallchart have been criticized on the grounds that they do not permit fair comparison between states. For example, the average SAT scores need to be corrected for the different proportions (largely due to self-selection) of the student population that take the test in each state, if comparison is to be meaningful (Wainer, 1986). Others would argue that socioeconomic differences between state populations also ought to be taken into account if the comparisons are to be fair (in the way that they have in school or school district comparisons in some US states [Salganik, 1990], and in school comparisons in the Inner London Education Authority in the UK [ILEA, 1990]). The publication of the Wallchart has stimulated a number of activities designed to improve upon the set of indicators displayed, and for that reason alone may be considered to have been a valuable impetus to improvement.

A more systematic approach is being followed by the Panel on Indicators established by the National Center for Educational Statistics in the USA. They are likely to recommend a thematic approach, with possibly different periodicities for updating; possible themes include:

the acquisition of knowledge and the engagement of the student in the learning process, readiness for entry to the school, and equity. Within the set of indicators for each theme, the indicators may be arranged in a pyramid, with a few key indicators at the top and many more in tiers below for those who want or need a more thorough analysis.

Alternative systematic approaches that limit the number of indicators see them as being created to give information about current policy issues (for example, the effectiveness of particular educational reforms) or about the attainment of particular goals or explicit targets. The targets set by the US President jointly with the State governors in 1990 (such as drug-free schools and the elevation of the USA to first position in the international league tables of school students' performance in mathematics and science by the year 2000) lend themselves to the creation of particular indicators. This is also the approach advocated by the proponents of institutional development planning, who see indicators as being the primary tool for evaluating the degree to which the particular targets chosen for a given development cycle are attained (for example, Osborne, 1990; Hargreaves *et al*, 1989).

A system of indicators based on the policy concerns of the day runs the risk, as Carley (1981) put it, 'of faddism, and over-concentration on social factors of passing interest at the expense of those not currently subject to influence and debate' (p. 126). Hogwood and Gunn (1984) took a similar view, advocating a more comprehensive approach, including indicators which, though they may not seem very important or subject to much change over time at the present time, may turn out to be 'sleepers' which suddenly become of more significance ten years into the future. Darling-Hammond also stresses the importance of creating indicators independent of the current policy agenda.

While understanding the desire of busy policy-makers and managers for a limited and simple set of indicators, and the researchers' desire for a parsimonious one, there are dangers that arise from keeping the set small. The greatest danger is that of corruptibility of the behaviour of those whose performance is being monitored. The best-known example is 'teaching to the test', commonly seen when the stakes are high, that is, when an individual's future hinges on his or her test result. Broader, and possibly deeper, education suffers when almost all effort is devoted to changing the indicator values for the better. Darling-Hammond therefore argues for a measure of redundancy in the information conveyed by an indicator set, so that if behaviour changes in respect to one indicator it will also affect other indicators (not necessarily for the better).

This principle was taken considerably further by McEwen and Hau

Chow (1991) to encompass different educational value systems and the different levels of education that each need different kinds of information. They argue for:

> the proposed strategy (that) might be called the multiplier effect:
>
> (i) multiple goals of education, based on appropriate dimensions and domains of schooling;
> (ii) multiple indicators of each goal measured by multiple methods;
> (iii) multiple levels of analysis: student, class, school, system, province, (and potentially) country, the world; and
> (iv) multiple participants: government, administrators, teachers, academics, parents.
>
> (McEwan and Hau Chow, 1991, p. 81).

While it is easy to see the value of such a set of indicators, there are other factors (notably feasibility and cost) that curtail the possibility of its development — one of many examples of how the different kinds of considerations (policy, technical and practical) come into conflict.

Nevertheless, policy considerations — indeed, the whole policy context — will always remain salient if the indicator system is to continue to be useful (as the fate of the social indicator system discussed above demonstrates). As McDonnell (1989) sees it:

> The policy context, then, plays two distinct roles in the design of an indicator system. First, it provides the major *rationale* for developing and operating such a system. Second, the policy context constitutes a key *component* of any educational indicator system, because specific policies can change the major domains of schooling in ways that affect educational outcomes. (pp. 241–2)

The Modelling Approach

The increased value of a system of indicators that reveals cause-and-effect relationships, that can therefore predict changes as a result of policy-makers' actions, is obvious, but not easy to achieve. Variables must be included in the model that are amenable to direct manipulation by the policy-maker and that link through some causal mechanism to effect the desired outcomes.

Choosing Indicators

Social and educational research has, over the years, provided much evidence of relationships between variables, sometimes causally linked but more commonly just associated, but no general model of the educational process, including all phases from pre-school to recurrent education, and for all kinds of different outcomes (intellectual, social and behavioural), currently exists. The review by van Herpen (1989) demonstrated how many different models have been put forward in educational research, and how incomplete and biased (towards one epistemological perspective) they are. The OECD Indicators Project adopted a broad framework based essentially on an input-output (i.e. economic) model of education (see below) and commentators were quick to draw attention to competing models, from which different indicator sets would be derived. Moreover, Bulmer (1990) claims that the theories and models in the realm of social indicators are all too general to provide an adequate starting point for the development of indicators.

Only econometric models are sufficiently detailed to be used to predict future behaviour (of the economy), but even then models provide different results and reflect the theoretical positions of the modellers. The policy-makers' expectations of such models may then be too high, destined for disillusionment before long. As Greenberger, Crenson and Crissey (1976), who reviewed the use of models in the policy process, put it,

> ... the effectiveness of policy modelling depends not only on the model and the modeller, but on the policymaker too. Increasing the usefulness of models as instrument for enlightening decision makers will require behavioral adjustments by the policymakers as well as by the modelers. (pp. 328–9)

If adequate models cannot be constructed, some organizing principles behind the indicator system are still needed, and the term 'framework' is commonly used to avoid implications of causes and effects. In the field of social indicators, for example, a structuring by programmes (for example, health, education, etc) is often used. Carley (1980) views this approach as cost effective and straightforward but warns:

> The chief danger is that the sometimes tenuous cause and effect relationships implicit in the indicators might go unnoticed by administrators who may overvalue the explanatory power of the indicators. (p. 194)

This danger is seen in the framework put forward by the RAND study on indicators for mathematics and science (Shavelson *et al*, 1987). It was constructed after study of the research literature, and appears to be a form of flowchart or model on account of the arrows. The text makes a very important caveat that might easily be missed:

> The relationships depicted in this figure, of course, do not constitute a model in either a strict predictive or causal sense. However, they can serve as a framework, showing logical linkages among elements of the schooling system. (Shavelson *et al*, 1987, pp. 10–11)

The general consensus is that our understanding of the educational process is not yet sufficient for the postulation of a model, but that we are in a position to create a framework that embodies our limited knowledge of some empirical relationships, and that begins to relate malleable variables (that is, variables that can be readily altered by the policy-makers) to desirable outcomes, *without* appearing to promise too much. The INES Project has moved cautiously in its development of a framework, for this reason among others. In its first phase, a very basic framework was employed. In its second phase this has been elaborated considerably, but again without arrows between the boxes which might imply causal relationships.

Thus the two approaches (the one derived from policy considerations and the other from the modelling of the educational process) can be united in the form of a framework, as long as no strong cause-and-effect relationships are inferred and as long as it is recognized that values (both political and epistemological) will have influenced both the general design of the framework and the particular indicator categories used.

Technical Issues

If there are difficulties in arriving at a general framework or model embracing policy-relevant concepts such as 'achievement in science' and 'quality of teaching', there are also problems in defining the concepts sufficiently precisely to allow measures (indicators) to be taken. The problems in this move from concept to measure are well-known in the social sciences: one concept can generate dozens of different indicators. Most concepts require detailed specification and clarification — for example, what sorts of skills (in what mix), applied to what facts

Figure 3.1: Linking elements of the educational system

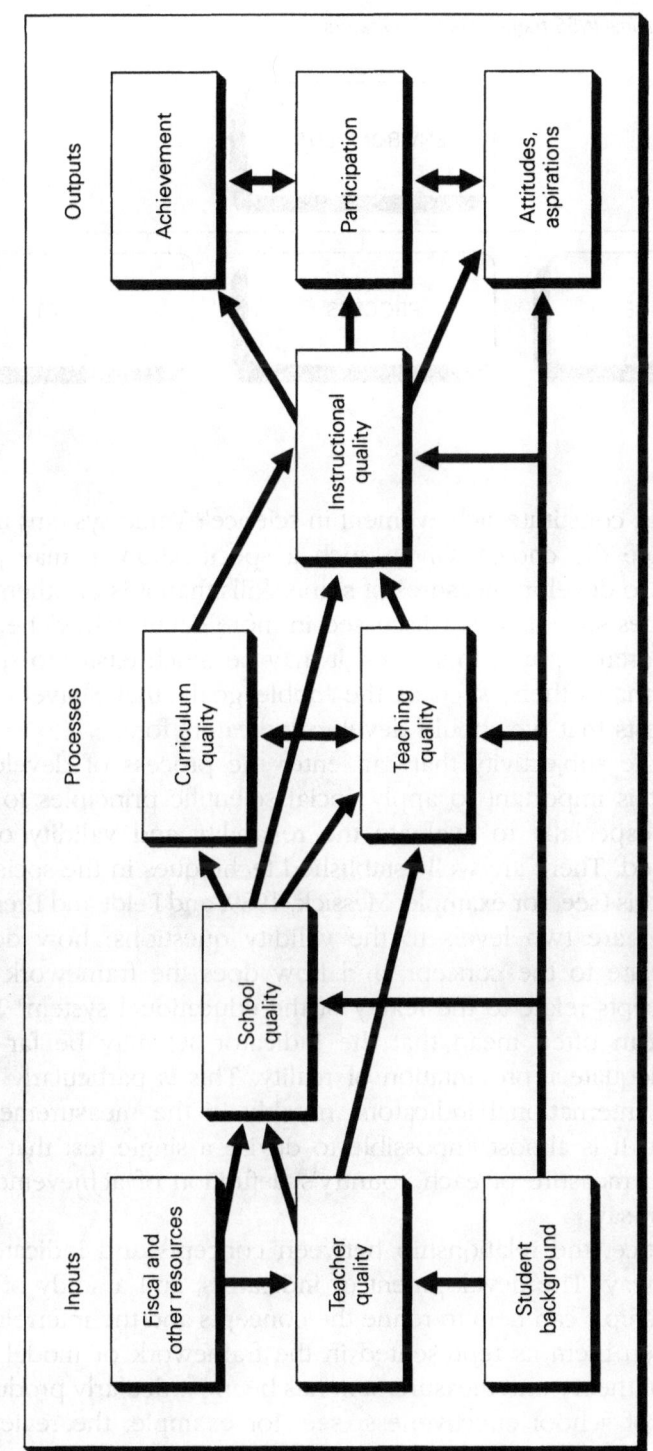

Source: Shavelson et al, 1987, p. 10.

Measuring Quality

Figure 3.2: *Original INES framework for indicators*

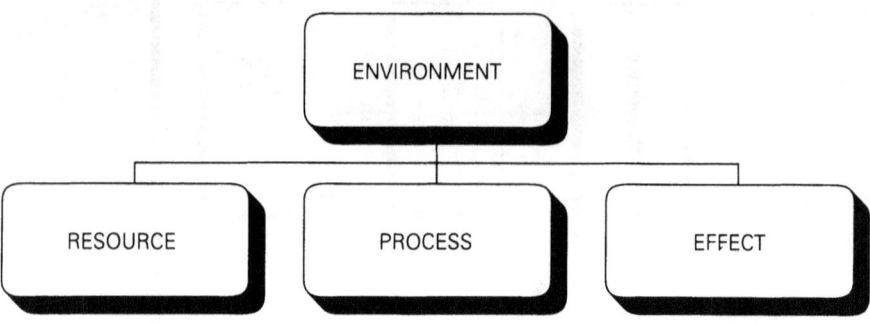

and concepts, constitute 'achievement in science'? Value systems inevitably influence the choice. Given such a specification, it may prove much easier to develop measures of some skills than it is of others, and practical issues such as cost (discussed in more detail below) begin to assume importance; and, moreover, it may be much easier to specify some skills than others, such as the 'noble goals' that Shavelson (in press) suggests that we should develop indicators for.

Given the subjectivity that can enter the process of developing indicators, it is important to apply social scientific principles to their evaluation, especially to evaluate the reliability and validity of the measures used. There are well-established techniques in the social sciences to do this (see, for example, Messick, 1989; and Feldt and Brennan, 1989). There are two levels to the validity questions: how do the measures relate to the concept, and how does the framework linking the concepts relate to the reality of the educational system? These two levels can often mean that the indicator set may be far from being an adequate representation of reality. This is particularly so in the case of international indicators, notably in the measurement of achievement. It is almost impossible to devise a single test that is an equally valid measure of each country's definition of achievement in mathematics, say.

In practice, the relationship between concepts and indicators is not all one way. The development of indicators, and a study of their interrelationships, can help to refine the concepts and the interrelationships between them as represented in the framework or model. This interaction of theory and measurement has been particularly productive in the field of school effectiveness (see, for example, the review by

Scheerens, 1990) and frequently leads to the development of composite or complex concepts. For example, the review of the literature on the influence of school context by Oakes (1989) led her to propose three general constructs of significance (all seen as *enablers* rather than causes of student learning): access to knowledge, press for achievement, and professional teaching conditions. All three are far from *simple*, and for each Oakes suggests that it would be necessary to measure at least nine 'more tangible school characteristics'. She does not propose whether or how the separate measurements should be combined to form a single indicator, or how the validity of the measures would be established.

The creation of composite indicators is likely to be important in indicator systems, if only to avoid overloading the reader with numbers. Social science and statistics can again offer well-tried techniques for forming homogeneous composite measures (for example, using factor analysis or other approaches to multi-dimensional scaling — see, for example, Mardia, Kent and Bibby, 1979), but they have rarely been applied in indicator systems (except in achievement and attitude measurement). Some have gone so far as to suggest a single composite indicator of the success of the educational system, namely the Gross Educational Product (analogous to the Gross Domestic Product, which is itself composed of a multitude of smaller measures). The former is not, of course, as simple as the latter, since education lacks the sort of common measure that economics employs (dollars or pounds sterling). The creation of a composite would therefore require the application of scaling and weighting techniques (see, for example, Petersen, Kolen and Hoover, 1989). In any case, even econometric modelling runs into difficulties when there is no direct and simple way of generating a monetary indicator, for example, for intangibles such as environmental pollution or for non-monetized activities such as household chores.

Nevertheless, the general thrust of research in education suggests that it is complex concepts of the kind synthesized by Oakes that are likely to have explanatory power; many of these may have to be appraised and measured by experts, such as inspectors, who may be able to arrive at numerical judgments of the relative 'quality of the learning environment' or 'professional teaching conditions' across different institutions. With such judgments, not only is validity an important concern but the reliability or consistency of judgment, between experts and over time, also becomes of great significance. Reliability of lower level indicators such as pupil-teacher ratio is more easily achieved, but is still a vital quality.

Measuring Quality

Practical Issues

To be useful to the policy-maker, indicators do not only have to be relevant but, experience shows, they must also be timely, comprehensible and few in number. Ensuring timeliness puts pressure on the indicator technicians who themselves may often be dependent on the actions of thousands of others in providing data (an activity to which those thousands may not attach much priority, not least because they often stand to gain little by carrying it out), and on the cost of the exercise: modern information technology and sampling both offer ways of streamlining procedures, but the cost of providing timely high quality information is likely to remain substantial. This is particularly true in the domain of student achievement measures.

Restricting the number of indicators probably assists in their gaining attention and being comprehensible, but may reduce the validity of the set of indicators as a framework representing the education system. Comprehensibility will be assisted by clear presentation, but many argue that the clearest-presented information still needs interpretative comment (for example, Odden, 1990) — the indicators do not 'speak for themselves'. Such interpretative comment will inevitably reflect the values of the commentator if it is to be other than bland, which can therefore lead to political difficulties over the provision of any comment. Social indicators fell into this trap in the USA which led to the commentaries being offered elsewhere (notably in the *Annals of the American Academy of Political and Social Sciences*) rather than beside the indicators, and they were therefore frequently not referred to.

Another desirable characteristic of indicators is that the data should be incorruptible, in other words not liable to deliberate alteration before they are collected. Achievement testing is particularly prone to such manipulation, for example, by schools' making sure that those of lower achievement are absent on the day of the test or by coaching the students for the test.

Who Chooses the Indicators?

The previous section has examined the various factors that might influence the way in which indicators and indicator systems might be chosen. It is apparent that these choices are inevitably influenced by the value systems of those making the choice, and need to reflect the interests of the policy-makers while also reflecting scientific understandings of how the educational system functions. This led MacRae to propose a 'technical community' that could bridge the gap between the policy-makers and the social scientists (see above). Others feel that the 'consumers' of education should also have a voice (see Riley, 1990). Pollitt (1986) warns that imposing a system of indicators from above will alienate those whose assistance and goodwill are needed in the enterprise, and advocates a pluralistic stance so that every interested party can contribute to the discussion before the system is finalized.

Thus the answer to the question 'Who chooses the indicators?' must be in large measure political (or reveal political values) and will inevitably be of significance to the process of the selection of indicators, and to the outcomes of that process. Many writers have attempted to recognize its importance, alongside political, technical and practical considerations, by creating a set of criteria than an indicator system, and individual indicators, should meet before they come into use.

Criteria for Choosing, Developing and Evaluating Indicators

These criteria differ according to political values, as well as according to the particular policy context, the particular educational system and to the particular level (for example, national, regional of local) under study. The principles that have been proposed for developing and evaluating indicators therefore vary, as do the safeguards against misinterpretation and misuse that have been advocated, but there is also much in common between the criteria proposed.

For the OECD INES Project, Nuttall (1989) proposed the following principles:

(a) indicators are diagnostic and suggestive of alternative actions, rather than judgmental;
(b) the implicit model underlying the indicators must be made explicit and acknowledged;
(c) the criteria for the selection of indicators must be made clear and related to the underlying model;
(d) individual indicators should be valid, reliable and useful;
(e) comparisons must be done fairly and in a variety of different ways (for example, with like groups, with self over time, and using dispersions and differences between sub-groups as well as averages);
(f) the various consumers of information must be educated about its use.

A further criterion, aimed at safeguarding against the punitive use of indicators, was originally proposed:

Control over data must remain with those who provide it. Desirable though such a criterion might ideally be, in the end it was not retained on the grounds that in an international project it could not be met. Apart from the more technical criteria, this list appears to be primarily concerned with lowering the expectations and increasing the sophistication of users.

Other criteria proposed by English writers have attempted to seek a pluralistic view of indicators to ensure that the community has a genuine stake in them. For example, Riley (1990) proposed the following set:

- The process of developing school indicators should ensure that all the partners in education have a sense of ownership in the indicators.
- Accessible to all the partners in education.
- Comparable throughout the authority (school district or local education authority).
- Linked to school ethos and objectives.
- Inclusive of both cognitive and non-cognitive outcomes.
- Implementable.
- Based on consumer evaluation of the education experience.

It is apparent that this set concentrates on school-level indicators, as does the set proposed by Gray and Jesson (1988):

1. The most important consideration relating to the construction of performance indicators is that they should directly measure or assess schools' performance. Many of the proposals we have encountered to date seem only directly related to actual performance.
2. They should be central to the processes of teaching and learning which we take to be schools' prize objectives.
3. They should cover significant parts of schools' activities but not necessarily (and certainly not to begin with) all or even most of them.
4. They should be chosen to reflect the existence of competing educational priorities; a school which did well in terms of one of them would not *necessarily* be expected (or found) to do well in terms of the others.

5 They should be capable of being assessed; we distinguish assessment here from measurement, which implies a greater degree of precision than we intend.
6 They should allow meaningful comparisons to be made over time and between schools.
7 They should be couched in terms that allow schools, by dint of their efforts and the ways in which they chose to organize themselves, to be seen to have changed their levels of performance; that is to have improved or, alternatively, to have deteriorated relative to previous performance and other schools.
8 They should be few in number; three or four might be enough to begin with. After some experimentation over a period of years one might end up with a few more.

Gray and Jesson went on to propose what those three indicators should in fact be, based on the research evidence from the school effectiveness literature:

Performance Indicator Focus		Key Questions to be Addressed	Answer Categories
	1(a)	Taking the school as a whole, what proportion of pupils made expected levels of progress over the relevant time period.*	all or most well over half about half well under half few
1 Academic Progress			
	1(b)	What proportion of pupils of: (i) below average (ii) average (iii) above average prior attainment made expected levels of progress over the relevant time period?*	all or most well over half about half well under half few
	2(a)	What proportion of pupils in the school are satisfied with the education they are receiving?	all or most well over half about half well under half few
2 Pupil Satisfaction			
	2(b)	What proportion of pupils of (i) below average (ii) average	all or most well over half about half

Measuring Quality

	(iii) above average attainment are satisfied with the education they are receiving?	well under half few
3(a)	What proportion of pupils in the school have a good relationship with one or more teachers?	all or most well over half about half well under half few

3 Pupil-teacher Relationships

3(b)	What proportion of pupils of: (i) below average (ii) average (iii) above average attainment in the school have a good relationship with one or more teachers?	all or most well over half about half well under half few

* Initially this question might be posed in terms of summary measures of pupil attainment; subsequently, more detailed breakdowns (subject-by-subject for example) might be attempted.

This set of indicators and the criteria that precede them see particular merit in the number of indicators being kept small, and the writers do not worry that the list only partially covers the goals of education (and certainly contains no redundancy). The indicators are chosen to focus on important goals, and pay no attention to processes and virtually none to context (only 1a and 1b, by using the term 'expected levels of progress', acknowledge the relativity of measures).

Criteria proposed in the USA tend to reflect primarily the concerns of policy-makers above the level of the school. Windham (1990) drew attention to the conclusions in the economic sphere that indicators should be 'accurate, relevant, timely, understandable and affordable'; Carley (1981) attributed the failure of the social indicators movement largely to the dominant influence of researchers who, in the search for accuracy, ignored relevance, timeliness and comprehensibility. Nevertheless, there had for some time been a recognition that these factors were important. For example, the US Urban Institute put forward the following criteria:

(1) *Appropriateness and validity*: indicators must be quantifiable, in line with goals and objectives for that service, and be oriented towards the meeting of citizen needs and minimizing detrimental effects;

(2) *Uniqueness, accuracy and reliability*: indicators generally need not overlap, double counting should be avoided, but some redundancy may be useful for testing the measure themselves;
(3) *Completeness and comprehensibility*: any list of indicators should cover the desired objectives and be understandable;
(4) *Controllability*: the conditions measured must be at least partially under government control;
(5) *Cost*: staff and data collection costs must be reasonable;
(6) *Feedback time*: information should become available within the time-frame necessary for decision-making.
(Hatry *et al*, 1977, quoted by Carley, 1981, p. 166)

Rockwell (1989) offers a rather similar list: timeliness, providing 'handles for policy', covering both current and emerging policy issues, in a time series, measures adaptable to changing circumstances, valid, reliable and accurate.

The most influential US proposals for criteria emerged from the RAND work on indicator systems for monitoring mathematics and science education (Shavelson *et al*, 1987, pp. 27–8). They were that indicators should:

- Provide information that *describes central features of the educational system* — for example, the amount of financial resources available, teachers' work load, and school curriculum offerings. Even though research has not as yet determined the relationship of some of these features to particular outcomes, information is needed about them to understand how the system works and because policymakers and the general public care about factors such as per pupil expenditures and class size.
- Provide information that is *problem-oriented*. Indicators must provide information about current or potential problems — for example, factors linked to teacher supply and demand, or to the changing demographics of urban areas.
- Provide information that is *policy-relevant*. Indicators should describe educational conditions of particular concern to policymakers and amendable to change by policy design. For example, indicators of teacher characteristics such as educational background and training are policy-relevant, since they can be changed through legislation or regulations governing teacher licensing.

Measuring Quality

- *Measure observed behaviour rather than perceptions.* Indicators will be more credible if they assess actual behaviour rather than participants' opinions or judgments. For example, the academic rigour of schools is better measured by course requirements and offerings than by principal, teacher, and student perceptions.
- *Provide analytical links among important components.* Indicators will be more useful if they permit the relationships among the different domains of schooling to be explored.
- Generate data from measure generally accepted as *valid and reliable*. Indicators should measure what they are intended to measure and should do so consistently.
- Provide information that can be *readily understood by a broad audience*. Indicators need to be easily comprehensible and meaningful to those beyond the immediate mathematics and science community — to policymakers, press, and the general public.
- Be *feasible* in terms of timeliness, cost and expertise. Indicator data need to be produced within a time frame that is compatible with policymakers' decision cycles and within given cost constraints; they should also be collectable, analysable, and reportable within current levels of expertise.

On the more technical side, this list is similar to the others (several of which it influenced, no doubt) but it again sees the policy-maker as the main client for indicator information.

Some of the differences between the lists are a function of the particular audience that the indicators are designed to address (for example, national policy-makers or school personnel) but other differences are less easy to resolve. There is broad agreement about technical and practical matters (for example, validity, reliability, timeliness, comparability, feasibility and keeping costs reasonable) and little difference on the need for policy relevance and the importance of ensuring that the indicators are comprehensible to their audience(s).

The major areas of difference are the number and the focus of the indicators. While most commentators recognize that the indicators (or at least some of them) should be alterable or controllable (by the actions of the policy-makers), they differ about their number, the need for redundancy, and the extent to which the indicators should be comprehensive and organized by and into a framework that embodies the functioning of the educational system, with, where possible, known causal links. Where the set is not comprehensive, there is agreement that it should focus on the central features and outcomes of the educational process.

It is therefore unavoidable that indicators cannot meet all the different criteria that have been proposed. The developers of an indicator set must resolve whether they are going to lean more towards a small number of key indicators or more towards a comprehensive set, embodying context and process as well as outcome. They will have to trade off one criterion at the expense of another, for example greater comprehensiveness against greater cost.

Conclusions

The lessons from the fate of social indicators must be learnt and applied to the development of educational indicators, while recognizing that even in the field of economics there is not a single accepted framework and that the results of economic predictions, using econometric models, are still contentious. Almost all the sets of criteria discussed above recognize the importance of policy-relevance and the inevitability of politicization.

This chapter has attempted to describe and analyse the cluster of interacting factors that influence the development of an indicator system. These factors are: (a) policy considerations, (b) research knowledge, (c) technical considerations, (d) practical considerations, and (e) the 'choosers' — those in a position to influence the choice and development of indicators.

Many have attempted to indicate, through the stating of criteria, how these factors can be translated into a set of principles for guiding the development of indicators, and the list below synthesizes some of the most important from among those discussed in the previous section:

- policy-relevant
- policy-friendly (timely, comprehensible and few in number)
- derived from framework (defensible in research terms, and including alterable variables, hence oriented towards action)
- technically sound (valid and reliable)
- feasible to measure at reasonable cost.

The nature and importance of these considerations will vary according to the locus or level of the action and the purpose of the system of indicators. For example, the framework and the potential action-points could be different for an indicator system led primarily by the concerns of national policy-makers from those for one designed for a local school system or an individual school site. The differences might be even more pronounced between a system designed to inform managers at the local level and a system designed for local accountability, which would tend to stress outcomes much more.

It also must be recognized that, whatever the level, these principles interact and sometimes conflict. Increases in validity rarely occur without increases in cost, and may well adversely affect timeliness. In the final analysis, then, the quality of the indicator system is likely to be crucially determined by those who hold the purse-strings, almost always the policy-makers on behalf of their constituents. It follows, first, that policy-relevance and policy-friendliness are likely to be of major significance, possibly at the expense of the 'scientific' validity of the framework. Second, fewer rather than more, indicators are likely to be preferred, again possibly at the expense of validity. Finally, the technicians will have to work closely with the policymakers, to ensure that expectations do not become so high that they are fated to turn into disillusionments, while nevertheless pointing to the potential, albeit limited, value of the development of an indicator system.

Acknowledgment

This chapter originates from the International Education Indicators Project of the OECD and appears in the OECD publication from that Project 'Education Counts'.

References

BULMER, M. (1990) 'Problems of theory and measurement', *Journal of Public Policy*, **9**, 4, pp. 407–12.
CARLEY, M. (1980) *Rational Techniques in Policy Analysis*, London, Heinemann Educational Books.
CARLEY, M. (1981) *Social Measurement and Social Indicators: Issues of Policy and Theory*, London, George Allen & Unwin.
CIPFA (1988) *Performance Indicators in Schools: A Contribution to the Debate*, London, CIPFA (The Chartered Institute of Public Finance and Accountancy).
FELDT, L.S. and BRENNAN, R.L. (1989) 'Reliability' in LINN, R.L. (Ed.) *Educational Measurement*, New York, American Council of Education/Macmillan Publishing Company (3rd edn).

GRAY, J. and JESSON, D. (1988) Personal communication.
GREENBERGER, M., CRENSON, M.A. and CRISSEY, B.L. (1976) *Models in the Policy Process*, New York, Russell Sage Foundation.
HARGREAVES, D.H., HOPKINS, D., LEASK, M., CONNOLLY, J. and ROBINSON, P. (1989) *Planning for School Development: Advice to Governors, Headteachers and Teachers*, London, Department of Education and Science.
HATRY, H.P. et al (1977) *How Effective are your Community Services: Procedures for Monitoring the Effectiveness of Municipal Services*, Washington, DC, The Urban Institute.
HOGWOOD, B.W. and GUNN, L.A. (1984) *Policy Analysis for the Real World*, Oxford, Oxford University Press.
INNER LONDON EDUCATION AUTHORITY (1990) *Differences in Examination Performance* (RS 1277/90), London, ILEA Research & Statistics.
INNES, J.E. (1990) 'Disappointments and legacies of social indicators', *Journal of Public Policy*, **9**, 4, pp. 429–32.
JAEGER, R.M. (1978) 'About educational indicators: Statistics on the conditions and trends in education', *Review of Research in Education*, **6**, pp. 276–315.
JOHNSTONE, J.N. (1981) *Indicators of Education Systems*, London and Paris, Kogan Page and UNESCO.
KINGDON, J.W. (1984) *Agendas, Alternatives, and Public Policies*, Boston, MA, Little, Brown.
MACRAE, D. Jr (1985) *Policy Indicators: Links Between Social Science and Public Debate*, Chapel Hill, NC, University of North Carolina Press.
MARDIA, K.V., KENT, J.T. and BIBBY, J.M. (1979) *Multivariate Analysis*, London, Academic Press.
MCDONNELL, L.M. (1989) 'The policy context' in SHAVELSON, R.J., MCDONNELL, L.M. and OAKES, J. (Eds) *Indicators for Monitoring Mathematics and Science Education: A Sourcebook*, Santa Monica, CA, RAND Corporation.
MCEWAN, N. and HAU CHOW (1991) 'Issues in implementing indicator systems', *The Alberta Journal of Educational Research*, XXXVII, **1**, pp. 65–86.
MESSICK, S. (1989) 'Validity' in LINN, R.L. (Ed.) *Educational Measurement*, New York, American Council of Education/Macmillan Publishing Company (3rd edn).
NISBET, J. and BROADFOOT, P.M. (1980) *The Impact of Research on Policy and Practice in Education*, Aberdeen, Aberdeen University Press.
NUTTALL, D.L. (1989) 'The functions and limitations of international educational indicators', paper prepared for the OECD/CERI INES Project, Paris.
OAKES, J. (1989) 'What educational indicators? The case for assessing school context', *Educational Evaluation and Policy Analysis*, **11**, 2, pp. 181–99.
ODDEN, A. (1990) 'Making sense of education indicators: 'The missing ingredient' in WYATT, T. and RUBY, A. (Eds) *Education Indicators for Quality, Accountability and Better Practice*, Sydney, Australian Conference of Directors-General of Education.
OSBORNE, D.A. (1990) 'The NSW school development and evaluation model' in WYATT, T. and RUBY, A. (Eds) *Education Indicators for Quality,*

Accountability and Better Practice, Sydney, Australian Conference of Directors-General of Education.

PETERSEN, N.S., KOLEN, M.J. and HOOVER, H.D. (1989) 'Scaling, norming and equating' in LINN, R.L. (Ed.) *Educational Measurement*, New York, American Council of Education/Macmillan Publishing Company (3rd edn).

POLLITT, C. (1986) 'Performance measurement in the public services: Some political implications', *Parliamentary Affairs*, **39**, 3, pp. 315–29.

RILEY, K. (1990) 'Making indicators consumer-friendly', *Education*, 11 May, pp. 470–2.

ROCKWELL, R.C. (1989) 'Lessons from the history of the social indicators movement', paper prepared for the NCES Indicators Panel, Washington, DC.

ROSE, R. (Ed.) (1990) 'Whatever happened to social indicators? A symposium', *Journal of Public Policy*, **9**, 4, pp. 399–450.

RUBY, A. (1990) 'Do common values produce common indicators? An illustration from the CERI project on international education indicators' in WYATT, T. and RUBY, A. (Eds) *Education Indicators for Quality, Accountability and Better Practice*, Sydney, Australian Conference of Directors-General of Education.

SALGANIK, L.H. (1990) 'Adjusting educational outcome measures for student background: Strategies used by states and a national example', paper prepared for the NCES Indicators Panel, Washington, DC.

SCHEERENS, J. (1990) 'School effectiveness research and the development of process indicators of school functioning', *School Effectiveness and School Improvement*, **1**, 1, pp. 61–80.

SELDEN, R. (1991) 'The INES framework', *The INES Handbook*, Paris, OECD.

SHAVELSON, R.J. (in press) 'Can indicator systems improve the effectiveness of mathematics and science education? The case of the US', *Evaluation and Research in Education*.

SHAVELSON, R.J., McDONNELL, L., OAKES, J., CAREY, N. with PICUS, L. (1987) *Indicator Systems for Monitoring Mathematics and Science Education*, Santa Monica, CA, RAND Corporation.

VAN HERPEN, M. (1989) 'Conceptual models in use for educational indicators', paper prepared for the OECD/CERI INES Project, Paris.

WAINER, H. (1986) 'The SAT as a social indicator: A pretty bad idea' in WAINER, H. (Ed.) *Drawing Inferences from Self-Selected Samples*, New York, Springer-Verlag.

WEISS, C.H. (1979) 'The many meanings of research utilization', *Public Administration Review*, **39**, pp. 426–31.

WINDHAM, D. (1990) Personal communication (comments made as discussant at symposium on OECD/CERI INES Project at AERA Annual Meeting, April 1990).

Chapter 4

How Indicators Have Been Used in the USA

Ramsay Selden

This chapter provides a brief chronological history of the development and use of educational indicators in the US. It goes on to review some of the issues and impact associated with the use of indicators in the US and argues that top-down testing needs to be linked to efforts to support school improvement.

Early National Efforts

In the US we have had some early national efforts at developing indicators in education. In the 1970s and earlier, we had movements to develop social indicators, usually in the spirit of the central planning movement. By the late 1970s and early 1980s, our Federal Department of Education and its National Center for Education Statistics had mounted a concerted program to develop a set of educational indicators and to issue an annual report entitled *The Condition of Education*.

1983 saw the watershed event of our National Commission on Excellence in Education releasing a report called *A Nation At Risk*. This not only spearheaded a reform movement that has yet to diminish, but also it stimulated a new look at the issue of educational indicators. Whereas the *Condition of Education* had been intended as a routine monitoring report, *A Nation At Risk* was analytical and evaluative, concluding that the education system was 'mediocre' and responsible for unacceptably low levels of student performance.

A Nation At Risk interpreted many available educational indicators in developing its conclusions. International achievement comparisons were made; trends in domestic testing programs were cited; teacher salary data and other indicators of school conditions were used; and explanatory data such as the courses students tended to take in high school were offered. That *A Nation At Risk* used indicator-type data in this way had two effects. One was to attract a massive amount of attention to the condition of education in the US, and to stimulate efforts at reform to improve those conditions. The other was to reveal how various kinds of statistical information, such as test results, and conclusions from various studies, could be interpreted as indicators of the conditions of the educational system. Trends in test scores, international studies, survey results and basic educational statistics, were analysed. This showed the way toward systematic, ongoing use of indicators in education, and the interest in reform stimulated by this report, provided the contextual support for continuing these efforts.

About a year after *A Nation At Risk*, the US Secretary of Education released the first of a regular series of 'league tables' comparing the states' educational performance. This was unprecedented in the US, and many, including the state chief education officers, complained about the chart. Surprisingly, this body, for whom I work, had endorsed going ahead with comparisons of the states on educational achievement, but they took issue with how the 'Wall Chart' handled them. The problems were the measures used — school leaving rates, which were not accurate, and college-aptitude test scores, which were not valid — and the lack of any contextualizing data reflecting the different socioeconomic conditions and challenges the states face. The chief state school officers also wanted information on the program input side, so they would know where to place their efforts to make things better.

Toward Current National Efforts

Critical to valid interstate comparisons was development of valid achievement measures. These had to address the profound question of whether enough consensus existed among state, local and classroom curricular emphases to base a single assessment and upon which to make comparisons. Another concern revolved around whether these assessments should reflect a current *status quo* or push the system somewhat by emphasizing ideals of performance that were beyond current practice.

We elected to use our National Assessment of Educational Progress (NAEP) for making achievement comparisons. NAEP had been used only to collect national and broad regional data that had no accountability implications. With agreement to use NAEP to compare states, the content and organization of its subject matter, the nature of its test exercises, the ancillary information that would be collected, and the use of the results all became critical. We have been engaged for the past five years in a planning and development effort to work out these features. In June 1991, the first state-by-state results were released, in eighth-grade mathematics.

By and large, this was a conscientious, successful endeavor, providing information and having consequences as one might have expected. Contextualizing information was made available in conjunction with the achievement results. We are not sure in the US whether we want to use this information to *adjust* results; we may wish just to start holding all schools to the same standard. The NAEP results (and other projects) also provide tremendously useful information on teachers' instructional coverage and practices. The June 1991 results, for example, found student performance associated with whether their teachers had studied more basic mathematics in college and whether they had had recent in-service professional development experiences in teaching mathematics.

We had a panel established by Congress to review all current activities in educational indicators and make recommendations on these efforts. This panel developed a model for educational indicators based not on background, inputs, and outputs (a process model), but on educational *issues* which indicators can inform. These issues have included equity, the contribution of education to productivity, readiness of young children for school, and others.

State Programs in Educational Indicators

Most of our fifty states and other territories are active in some way in operating programs of educational indicators. I would like to describe some of these programs as examples. The state programs might be conceived as falling into three categories: *indicator systems, report cards and accountability systems*.

In a survey conducted in 1990, we found that most states operate what they characterize as educational 'indicators systems'. These are statistical reporting programs representing key aspects of the education system. They are regularly reported for the state as a whole, for individual schools, or for school districts (which operate school systems at the local or municipal level in the US). The states of Connecticut and Nevada have been fairly typical in their indicator systems. They produce statewide and school-district data on achievement test outcomes, graduations rates, attendance and some school inputs, such as pupil-teacher ratios.

Over the past four-five years, several states have begun what they call school 'report cards'. 'Report cards' in the US are the means by which students receive their school grades or results. That is the term we use for the form by which they receive their results. We have applied the term to school reporting to connote the issuing of 'grades' on the schools themselves. California pioneered this practice, beginning several years ago to release the results of its achievement testing program by school and expanding the practice to generate an annual school profile with test results, other outcome data, socioeconomic factors, and selected program inputs. Illinois, Louisiana and several other states have set out to design school report cards from the start. Louisiana conceived a three-layered system wherein a brief report would be made to the public on individual schools (a fold-out with key information on the school); an intermediate report would be designed on school district results; and a statewide report would hold the state itself accountable for educational goals.

The third type of state program is the accountability reporting system. Here, use of the data goes beyond public reporting. Some tangible reward or incentive is associated with it. In South Carolina, monetary awards to the school (but not necessarily to the teaching staff) are based on performance results. Conversely, poor results can trigger administrative sanctions, including removal of administrators and takeover of the schools. Other accountability systems include other rewards and sanctions, such as public recognition of the school or freedom from administrative regulations.

In these accountability systems, the structuring of incentives is tricky. The most benign and constructive positive incentive appears to be recognition. In our current climate of public interest and concern for reform, it is a powerful motivator. It is felt to be appropriate professionally, while still adapting accountability principles from the private sector. Many would like to link such accountability reporting to choice of schools by parents, which is not generally available among public schools in the United States.

Deregulation has a problem similar to that faced by cash incentives. If it is used to reward systems or schools that are doing well, the 'rich get richer', and schools that might need deregulation in order to make a fresh start are denied it. It does have the advantage of removing regulatory approaches from places that appear to be working well. In the US, it is felt that we have focused too much attention on regulation of inputs, such as the presence of libraries or fully certified teachers, rather than the outputs of schooling.

Monetary incentives are felt by many to be less appropriate professionally in education and to have the problem of rewarding the successful with even more resources. Further, monetary awards can put so much pressure on the data on which they are based as to result in distortions. Louisiana deliberately delayed initiation of a reward system based on its indicators program until the data collection and reporting could have time to become standardized, accurate and established in the local school systems.

There is a recent movement in the US to combine decentralization of decision-making (professionalization of teaching and site-based management of schools) with outcome-based accountability reporting. The idea is that schools would be monitored for their results, and that we would not be concerned about how the results are obtained, that the local staff could use its own ideas and initiative to achieve them.

There are two other purposes to which state and local indicator systems can be put in the US. One is to support analysis and planning. In New York, performance results are used to locate low-performing schools. These schools are required to plan an improvement strategy. This strategy is then monitored by the state to ensure its implementation and the local district is supported to carry it out. In Michigan, local districts are required to review the results of testing programs and other statistics and to develop plans based on them.

The final use, ostensibly, would be detailed diagnosis of the state's and local school systems' educational programs. This is a theoretical application of educational indicators. None in the US is sufficiently comprehensive, detailed, or valid to support that use.

Local Educational Indicator Programs

As mentioned earlier, local governments in the US actually operate the school systems. They have reported and used educational indicators in a limited way.

The most prevalent local role has been reporting of comparative achievement test results for the various schools. This is a fairly common practice, and is used to a degree by parents to decide where to live or to exert pressure on the school system to improve some schools. Virtually no other data are reported with these results, which are typically displayed in local newspapers, except that student aptitude levels or socioeconomic measures might be reported in a few cases. Most of the results reported by local school systems come from statewide testing and statistical programs.

Some states, such as Maryland, have established goals or standards for the schools, and local papers are beginning to report the numbers

Measuring Quality

of schools meeting these goals or standards. The standards include student assessment results, school leaving rates, attendance and other measures.

Recent National Developments

Until 1989 the United States was viewed as a strongly decentralized education system. The states and localities firmly maintained autonomy and responsibility for operating the schools and determining their curricula. The federal government staunchly avoided interfering in educational curriculum decisions. In 1989 the US decided to establish national goals in education for the first time. National 'goals' were seen as an appropriate way to set some central, national focus, which was seen as necessary to bring about needed improvements in education. To summarize, the goals are that, by the year 2000:

- all young children will come to school ready to learn;
- ninety per cent will complete secondary school;
- students will master challenging subject matter in the academic subjects of English, mathematics, science, history, and geography;
- US students will become first in the world in mathematics and science performance;
- adults will be literate and possess the knowledge needed to compete in a global economy and to exercise responsible citizenship; and
- all schools will be free of drugs and violence and offer a safe, disciplined environment for learning.

During 1990, measures were identified for each of these goals, and plans were developed for reporting on the status of the country toward reaching the goals. In the area of student learning or achievement, national standards for subject matter learning were envisioned, with systems of European-style exit examinations for students and program assessments to monitor schools and school systems, both keyed to these subject matter frameworks and standards. New measures were put forth for consistently and accurately measuring school-leaving rates: a voluntary, national student record system was proposed to assist this. New data collections were also proposed to track the experiences of young children before coming to school. And, commitments were made to participate in upcoming international comparisons of educational achievement.

How Indicators Have Been Used in the USA

The US is now moving towards some sort of quasi governmental body to promulgate standards by subject area for elementary secondary education and to moderate a national testing system to test student performance against the standards. As part of this process the National Assessment of Educational Progress has established absolute substantive standards of what students would be expected to learn. Prior to that, it was only a descriptive and normative testing program.

This effort is an accountability approach, using top-down testing and reporting of indicators to try to bring about change. However, there is no concurrent effort to provide support for improvement of schools. Most of us feel that massive amounts of 'unprecedentedly' effective professional development of teachers is needed to bring about significant changes in student learning. No such effort is part of the program. Whether the system can be moved only through public reporting and accountability is questionable. At the very least, it cannot be moved as quickly as if carefully targeted program support had been provided.

Impact of Indicators on Educational Programs — The US Experience

There can be no doubt that indicators have had an effect on the education system in the US — both positive and negative. The US is probably the most data-based education system in the world, we are certainly out front in our confidence in the value of student testing data and other measures for planning and accountability. Let me review some of the effects.

The analysis of indicators in our premier educational reform report — *A Nation At Risk* — contributed singularly to its effectiveness. The report was made compelling and acquired drama by using figures to portray the urgency of the US situation. Others learned how to use numbers in that way to maintain attention to the crisis of American education. These effects can be argued to be both positive and negative, negative in the sense of contributing to a little hysteria and carelessness.

Our student testing data have had both positive and beneficial effects. During the 1970s, the National Assessment of Educational Progress revealed that, in reading and mathematics, students were far more proficient in low-level aspects of reading and mathematics and relatively unproficient in the higher-order aspects of these subjects. These findings resulted in major reforms in curriculum and teacher education, both of which have been substantially redirected to reasoning and problem-solving in mathematics and critical comprehension in reading.

On the down side, most of our testing programs are oriented toward low-level, basic skills and rely heavily on multiple-choice questions. As we have put pressure on these scores, instruction has tended to collapse toward the tested skills and test-taking strategies. We are now working very hard to change our tests so they reflect the full breadth of the desired curriculum, including the deep, sophisticated aspects of learning that have eluded testing in the past. This is requiring the use of open-ended questions, performance tasks, and portfolios of student work in the new tests. Most of our new accountability programs are intent on using reformed tests of this nature.

State accountability systems have also experienced some of the down-sides in overreliance on test data. Public recognition has proved to be sufficiently desirable to result in some educators cheating on testing programs in order to obtain it. This problem is not widespread, but still unsettling. On the plus side, there is evidence in South Carolina, for example, that strong accountability systems have brought up the 'floor' in educational achievement, reducing the problems in the worst cases.

Conclusion

Shaw is reported to have said that the truly educated person is moved by statistics. This is an interesting notion, implying that the educated person understands and feels the depth of human experience behind the numbers, and that numbers convey the nature and scale of the human condition. This notion is important in using indicators in education; they are legitimate only if they are accompanied by sensitivity to the realities that numbers can mask.

The experience of the US with educational indicators prompts one to ask whether Shaw's observation can be turned around. Can statistics move education? To some extent, apparently, both positively and negatively. But whether indicators and statistics on their own can move school performance as much as we need to move it remains unknown.

Chapter 5

Quality, Surveillance and Performance Measurement

Kieron Walsh

Introduction

The changes in public sector management that have been introduced over the last few years are intended to create services that are more sensitive to the needs of the consumer, and in which providers are more accountable for performance. The logic of the approach, as laid out, for example, in the Citizen's Charter, is that the quality of public services will be improved by stating standards and setting objectives, measuring performance against targets, and taking remedial action where necessary. Wherever possible, markets or quasi-markets will be created so that citizen-consumers can exit from the service, just as they would exit if dissatisfied with something produced in the private sector and sold on the market. Citizens as consumers will then be able to make informed choices about the services that they receive, and producers will respond to the decisions of citizens in the way that private producers respond to customers in the market.

Accurate information on the services to be provided and on performance is central to the operation of the new market-oriented public service. The result is intended to be a public service that is more transparent to the public, and one in which the pressure of public opinion and choice will provide the incentive to continual service improvement.

The search for means of assessing the efficiency and effectiveness of public services, such as the education service, involves more than technical questions about the development of appropriate measures. It also involves issues of the distribution of power within public service organizations, and particularly the distribution of power between managers and professionals, between levels of government, and between public service organizations and the citizen. The development of performance measures involves fundamental questions about the nature of accountability within the public sector. The debate over performance management in the public services is a debate about the character of the public realm itself, and raises a number of issues that are central to the future character of public service management.

In this chapter I shall analyze the nature of the debate over performance measurement and management in the public service and its implications for the character of the public service. I shall start by considering the development of attempts to measure performance in the public sector over the past twenty-five to thirty years. In the next section I consider the key issues that arise in the measurement of performance and the major difficulties that are involved. These issues and difficulties create the need for an approach to the measurement of performance that is appropriate to the complexities involved, to the purposes of measurement, and to the nature of the public realm. I shall argue that what is emerging is a surveillance based approach to performance, in which trust and ambiguity is being reduced to a minimum, which is in conflict with the need for responsive systems that can cope with change and uncertainty, and which are based on a clearly developed ethic of public service. The surveillance approach is based upon the assumption that those in control can clearly define the work that is to be done by subordinates, and can monitor performance by checking the output against stated targets. Performance measurement, if it is to be developmental rather than controlling, must create the possibility of dialogue and debate, rather than attempt to create the conditions for an authoritarian judgment.

The Development of Performance Measurement

The concern to measure performance is part of the pursuit of rational managerialism that has long characterized the public sector. Approaches such as policy-planned-budgeting-systems (PPBS) and policy analysis and review (PAR) had a strong performance focus at the level of public services as a whole. From the late 1960s, the measurement of individual performance and the introduction of bonus systems for manual workers changed the nature of staff management in an attempt to relate performance to productivity. Reports, such as that of the Fulton Commission, emphasized the importance of performance measurement.

> Accountable management means holding individuals and units responsible for performance measured as objectively as possible. Its achievement depends upon identifying or establishing accountable units within government departments — units where

output can be measured as objectively as possible and where individuals can be held personally responsible for their performance. (Fulton, 1968, p. 51)

This statement would not be out of place in any number of reports of the 1980s or 1990s. What has been different about the last decade is not only that the measurement of performance has been pursued more consistently and vigorously, but that it has gone along with a significant shift in power in public sector organizations, and that it has been linked with the development of markets and control, rather than planning.

The shift in power involves the attempt to replace professional dominance with managerial control. The assertion of the priority of management may be accomplished through establishing new managerial positions, such as the general managers introduced in the National Health Service as a result of the Griffiths Report (Department of Health and Social Security, 1983), or the heads of agencies in the Civil Service; by requiring professionals to become managers, as has been done through the development of local management of schools in education; and, finally, through the introduction of managerial processes, such as the Financial Management Initiative in the Civil Service, or the Resource Management Initiative in the National Health Service. Whichever approach is used, the purpose is to ensure that there is a clearer evaluation of the relationship between means and ends, and between outcomes and the activities of individuals. Wherever possible, the relationship is to be analyzed and understood in quantitative terms.

In the 1980s, the performance emphasis developed rapidly, with the number of performance indicators growing from seventy in the National Health Service in the early 1980s to 450 in 1988 (Flynn, 1992, p. 109) and in the public expenditure white papers from 500 in 1985 to 1800 in 1987, after which 'no one was counting any more' (Carter *et al*, 1992, p. 20). Performance management and performance measurement and review systems were established in many local authorities. Performance pay was increasingly introduced for public sector staff.

Where the proposals for change in the 1960s and 1970s were based upon notions of comprehensive rational planning, those of the 1980s were based on market thinking that was fundamentally suspicious of the role of the planner. The reorganizations of local government and the National Health Service in the 1970s went along with the introduction of comprehensive planning processes that proved to be cumbersome and unwieldy, and unable to cope with the changes that began in the second half of the decade, as the public sector faced increasing financial difficulties. The market thinking that has dominated the last decade and more is based upon the argument that planning can never replace the market because it is dependent upon the availability of massive amounts of information, the capacity to process it, and time to do so. None of these characteristics are likely to be present in times of rapid change and uncertainty, and in any case the processes are too expensive. The performance emphasis of the 1980s is one that is to be attained through incentives and managerial control rather than planning.

Quality, Markets and Citizenship

The development of performance-based systems of management in the public sector has, more recently, come to be associated with three wider movements; the pursuit of quality, the development of market processes, and the enhancement of citizenship. There has long been criticism of the quality of the public service, a criticism which is easy to make because the concept itself is so slippery. The approach to quality that is being developed in the public sector focusses upon working in accordance with prior specifications, which is an engineering-based approach to quality. The nature of the product to be created or the activity to be carried out is laid down in more or less detail, and the test of quality is concerned with how much that specification has been met. It is this approach that lies behind the pursuit of certificated quality assurance systems. The approach is one of standardization and formalization of the product and the method of working. Products and services that are amenable to such an approach can be tested by inspectors, through quality assurance systems, and these inspectors need have little day-to-day contact with the services that they inspect. The tendency, in such approaches, is for the service or product to be defined by the expert rather than by the consumer or user.

The development of the National Curriculum, with regular testing of pupils on a standardized basis, is an example of such an approach. The debate on the nature of the curriculum and the form of tests to be used has taken place on an abstracted plane, and in terms that have little meaning to those who must use the system. The development of market approaches such as competitive tendering for services, and the expansion of choice, based upon a clear view of quality, is also premissed on the ability to assess performance. In the case of competitive tendering there are specifications against which performance can be assessed, and which allow the purchaser or client to take action, for example by deducting payment should it be inadequate. If people are to make informed choices between the services offered by the public service, so that market and quasi-market processes can be introduced, they must be able to assess the alternatives in terms of performance. Citizenship is then enhanced because the individual service user is able to put pressure on the public services, and hold them accountable through the exercise of informed choice. It may be that there is a need for specialists to evaluate certain aspects of service, or create the information for the citizen, but the operation of market-based citizenship depends upon effective information.

Performance information, as the basis on which the consumer-citizen chooses, is at the heart of the Citizen's Charter and the various service charters that have followed it. The Citizen's Charter is based upon seven principles of public service: standards, openness, information, choice, non-discrimination, accessibility, and redress. It is argued that:

> Full, accurate information should be readily available, in plain language, about what services are being provided. Targets should be published, together with full and audited information about the results achieved. Wherever possible, information should be in comparable form, so that there is pressure to emulate the best. (Prime Minister, 1991, p. 5)

It is difficult to argue against such a general aspiration, but whether or not it is possible to develop such simple measurement systems for performance is an empirical matter. The problems that are inherent in measurement cannot be overcome by an act of will.

The Limits of Measurement

It is not axiomatic that we should measure the performance of public service agencies at all. It may be impossible to do so, or the cost may not be worth the outcome. It makes perfect sense to say that it is worth providing a particular service in a particular way because it may have a beneficial effect, even though it may not be possible, either before or after the event to determine whether or not it actually worked. Where the purpose is prevention, for example, in health or social care, then it may be difficult to know whether it is one's actions or other factors which have been the causal influences. The relationship between cause and effect may be extremely difficult to determine, as will frequently be the case in education and in other complex public services. We will often make decisions on the basis of probabilities, or even possibilities,

Measuring Quality

for example that a particular approach to teaching or to community or health care is the most appropriate. The costs of information collection are likely to be particularly high in the public sector because of the difficulty in clearly defining purposes, the existence of externalities, the non-material nature of the majority of services, the complexity of many of the production processes, and the dispersed nature of production.

The difficulty in defining the public purpose is not technical, but is based in the nature of the public realm as the site of conflicting values. There are always differences in the values that people hold over what they want the public service to attain, which cannot simply be overcome by the will to measurement. We must recognize the public realm as one in which the multiplicity of values must be accepted because it is of the nature of politics that different value positions are perfectly valid and must be reconciled without destructive conflict. Complex human systems require practical wisdom in evaluation, and the exercise of good judgement rather than, or as well as, precise measurement (Williams, 1985). The comparison of values against one another is difficult even in the case of simple material goods such as cars or toothpaste. Marketers and economists have developed approaches to try to deal with these difficulties, such as conjoint analysis and hedonics, involving complex statistical manipulations (Kotler, 1988: Deaton and Muellbaker, 1980), though with limited success. In the public realm the difficulties are greater because we are concerned with basic human values, rather than the attempt to develop effective comparative measures of material attributes.

Interaction Effects

Many services are provided in the public service because they are characterized by significant externalities, where the activities of one person or organization produce effects for others that are not effectively accounted for in market transactions. In such instances, cost-benefit analysis will be difficult to make, and will tend to involve the comparison of incommensurable values. It may be possible for one individual or organization systematically to improve its performance against a given performance standard, but only by making effective performance more difficult elsewhere in the social system. For example, hospitals may increase their technical efficiency by discharging patients more rapidly, thereby creating housing problems and problems for those agencies providing care in the community, as has happened as a result of the closure of long-stay psychiatric institutions. Similar effects may follow from the exclusion of pupils with special needs or exhibiting disruptive behaviour from schools.

It will always be easier for individuals or agencies to achieve targets if they can increase their discretion by reducing that which is available to others. Where a service is characterized by externalities then the performance analysis net will need to be thrown widely, and involve judgment as much as measurement. The more complex the system, that is the more phenomena are linked to each other, the more likely it is that externalities will occur. It is consequently necessary to consider the performance of the system and not simply individual providers and providing organizations within that system. It is especially necessary to do so where organizations must work together to produce an effective service, as in the case of community care which depends upon the interaction of the National Health Service, social services and other local authority departments, social security, and voluntary agencies, amongst others.

Services to People

Services, whether they are provided on the market or through the public sector, are different from material goods. They are intangible, and consequently are not amenable to being stored or sampled for physical testing. Services do not persist over time, but are produced in what Normann (1985) calls the 'moment of truth'. The simultaneity of production and consumption means that it is difficult to measure directly many aspects of service performance. Services are also commonly produced in direct contact with the user, who must frequently contribute to the quality of what is produced, as in education, social care and health services. The measurement of performance must take account of the part that is played by the users and the initial endowments with which they come to the service. The more the service involves the user as a person then the less it is possible to assess the quality of service without taking into account the evaluations of the user.

Measurement of performance in service industries is complex because it is difficult to ensure that we are measuring comparable objects, or even to know what measurement would mean. It is difficult to be clear, for example, on what we mean by care for others. One of the benefits of the move towards more clearly stated standards and measurement of performance is likely to be that we examine what we are doing and try to assess whether it is meeting its purpose, but that is likely to be a long and difficult process for human services.

Production processes in the public sector are frequently complex and unclear. Standardization of services that are concerned with people, and often specifically with their individuality, is difficult, as attempts to standardize medical or educational procedures have shown. The professional nature of the public services follows partly from the fact that it is difficult to standardize the product or the production process and therefore to apply Taylorist approaches. The approach has been to develop the skills and experience possessed by individual professionals so that they will be able to act appropriately when faced with varying circumstances.

Part of the present development in the management of the public service is the attempt to standardize through definitions of service and statements of clear standards. The development of the National Curriculum, with specified standards and performance measurement, is a clear example of such an approach. It is difficult to achieve targets, especially where even those who are involved in the process of service production may not always be clear on what works and what does not, or on why they do certain things and not others. The danger of the search for the standardization of performance is that it ignores the responsive and creative element of professionalism. The need for services to be provided in close contact with the public also means that they are produced on dispersed sites. It is difficult to produce measurement systems that deal effectively with this dispersion, and ensure that one is comparing like with like, for example in comparing an inner-city school with one in a shire county.

Even if it is possible to measure the effectiveness of particular public services it may not be ethical to do so. It may not be acceptable to carry out the studies that would show us the effectiveness of a particular activity, because, for example, it may not be acceptable to experiment on people. It is often the case that we cannot effectively test medical approaches because we cannot experiment on people. The same is true, to a lesser extent, of services such as education, social care and social security. Where direct measurement and experimentation are difficult then we are thrown back onto secondary indicators, which will require care in interpretation. The ethics of the public service also tend to result in elements of inefficiency, in the care that is needed to treat people fairly and to ensure that public organizations are open to scrutiny. The democratic process is likely to take longer to reach decisions than does the dictator. Bureaucracy and democracy go together to a considerable degree.

Realistic Measurement

The argument that there are difficulties in measuring the performance of public services is not a counsel of despair, but a plea for realism, and for an attempt to develop measures that are appropriate to the nature and complexity of the phenomena being measured. We are required to act even if we cannot be certain of the appropriateness of our actions or of what the results will be. We must, in many circumstances, act on the balance of probabilities, and on the basis of whatever understandings we are able to develop, however inadequate. It may be necessary to take action now to avoid potential problems in the future even though our knowledge of cause and effect is limited, for example, in trying to prevent potential future environmental problems. It is dangerous to assume that we should not take action to deal with the greenhouse effect because it has not yet been proved.

Equally, however, it is inappropriate and, perhaps, unfair to relate reward to performance if we are unable to develop very clear understandings of the causes of effectiveness. Those who are effective may be so purely by chance, with little idea of how they achieve what they do. Momentum may ensure continuing success by those who simply started in the right way or in the right place, and effective performance may have little to do with the efforts of those who achieve as against those who do not. There is little point in relating reward to performance if it can have no influence on performance, and is not related to the merit of the performer.

The Purposes of Measurement

Technical Control

Where we can measure performance, and it is worth the cost of doing so, there may be a number of purposes. The first and most obvious is control. The measurement of performance may yield technical control, by acting as a feedback mechanism, and enabling us to adjust our activities to achieve better results. This is what Carter (1989) defines as using performance measures as dials, which tell us how the system is performing and allow fine-tuning. Such performance measurement will normally involve absolute measures and is relatively uncontentious. However, even such absolute measures require interpretation if they are to be used effectively. They will need to be judged against something. We may know levels of background radiation, or the speed of vehicles, or the number of children absent from a school, but we will still have to interpret that information, if we are to decide how to act on it.

The fact that we can make an absolute measure of performance does not mean that we can do anything to change it, though knowing the size of the problem may allow us to plan. We may be able to measure climate and weather, but we can do little to change them in the short term. We can though act in the light of that knowledge, for example, to create appropriate buildings. Even in the case of absolute measures we must be able to interpret them effectively and be clear whether it is possible to bring about change in the measure, or simply adjust our behaviour on the basis of it.

Performance and Reward

Performance measures, where they can be related to effort, may be used to devise incentive and reward systems that provide semi-automatic control systems. This approach is increasingly being used to tie pay to performance for public service managers. Competition is being used to target the use of grants by central government on those local authorities seen as being able to use them most effectively, for example in housing where those systems that are seen as performing well are rewarded with relatively favourable grant settlements. The more easily we can relate outcome to effort, the easier it will be to manage from a distance. There are clear dangers in such an approach. The Audit Commission, in its study of the strategic housing role of local authorities, questioned the distribution of housing finance on the basis of performance:

> It is therefore important that the enhanced element of discretion in HIP (Housing Investment Programme) allocations does not create incentives for authorities to pursue particular activities such as shared ownership, regardless of their relevance to local needs. If competition steers resources from needy authorities to authorities which are efficient but which do not face housing problems, this new approach will not solve the country's housing problems. An emphasis on needs remains important, but the measurement of them is currently flawed. (Audit Commission, 1992, p. 34)

There is certainly a clear difference and, almost certainly, a conflict between reward on the basis of performance, and distribution according to need. The linking of reward to performance measurement will tend to bias systems towards improving achievement on the particular measure, perhaps at the expense of other activities that are equally, if not more important. There are also many studies that show the way that performance bonus systems will lead to resorting to the 'sharp pencil' to earn one's income rather than increasing effort. It may be much easier in the case of education testing for the school to keep out those who are likely to drive the score down, than to try to improve their performance. Generally those who are subject to performance measurement will decide either to improve their performance, or to change the factors that will influence the measurement of performance independently of their performance. The more able they are to influence the independent determinants of performance the less effective performance measurement will be.

The Icarus Paradox

The use of absolute measures of performance, particularly when combined with the 'excellence' movement (Peters and Waterman, 1982), may lead to an excessive focus on some aspects of the work of an organization at the expense of others. Miller (1990) has recently shown how this narrowing of the organizational focus can lead to what he calls the Icarus paradox, by which successful organizations, by overemphasizing the successful dimensions of their operation, can fail. The pioneering technological organization, for example, can become utopian, engaging in high tech fantasies; the well controlled organization can become excessively bureaucratized. Again, the pioneering innovating organization, measuring, say, the number of patents or new product ideas, may fail to take account of the extent to which new ideas fail. Measurement that reflects the character of the organization can contribute to such an effect, overemphasizing certain features at the expense of balance and variety. Corporate failures can frequently be seen to have resulted from such one-sided developments.

Performance-based rewards are unlikely to be effective where achievement has little to do with the activity of the person rewarded. Senior managers are frequently rewarded with stock options which are intended to encourage them to act in ways that will improve the performance of the organization's stock, when there is no very clear causal relationship between the action and outcome. A recent example of this is the case of the privatized public utilities such as British Telecom and the water companies, where performance-related rewards have been considerable, but it is difficult to envisage the circumstances in which they could have failed to have been achieved, given the conditions of the sale and the monopoly character of the market.

Improving Service Provision

Performance measurement may also be used to provide the basis for the development of more effective service provision, through providing data for analysis and dialogue. This would require a degree of responsiveness to the user and acceptance of a measure of inefficiency. Responsiveness is necessary since any concept of purpose must rely on the user's understanding of need and effectiveness in the case of complex human services. Inefficiency follows from the requirement to change in response to varying circumstances, and the consequent need to learn a new set of activities, disrupting previously learned patterns of action. In a world of complexity and uncertainty it is unlikely that it will be possible to lay down detailed service specifications that will not require constant modification and change. The skill that is needed is one of judgment rather than of measurement — the ability to assess ambiguous situations, and to form and weigh alternative courses of action. Because circumstances will continually differ it will be necessary to change and adapt, and the skill that is required is the ability to read and adapt to circumstances, not follow a specification.

The operation of the market depends upon the ready availability of information on quality, and the ability to act on it, preferably by exiting from the market. Where the cost of quality measurement is very high, as for example in the case of uncut diamonds (Kenney and Klein, 1983) or wholesale fish (Wilson, 1980), then particular types of market emerge based upon trust and reputation. It may be difficult for the professional to demonstrate superior quality, making investment in better service difficult, because an appropriate price cannot be charged (Dingwall and Fenn, 1987). If consumers cannot assess the quality of a service then they will either assume that all providers are the same, or decide on the basis of criteria that do not actually reflect quality, such as price.

The availability of information on quality is crucial to the ability of the consumer to form judgments on alternative providers. Evidence from the United States of America on the operation of markets in health shows that costs tend to rise where it is difficult to assess quality, because hospitals invest in expensive equipment, intended to serve as a sign of quality, and keep beds empty so that doctors will feel able to refer patients (Culyer and Posnett, 1990). More generally, market mechanisms work only with difficulty where there are significant quality issues in the evaluation of the product (Hirschman, 1970), differences between the information that is available to user and producer, and differences of incentive between principal and agent (Ross, 1973).

Allocating Responsibility for Failure or Success

There is a problem in judging the quality of performance where it is difficult to assess whether failure is the result of the action of the service provider, of the consumer, or of the state of the world. In the case of simple material goods it is generally fairly easy to assign blame; for public services it is more difficult. Education and medicine provide obvious examples. It is obvious that some doctors and hospitals, or some teachers and schools, will be better than others, but it will often not be easy to tell which is which. The action of the user, the patient or the student will clearly have an influence on outcomes, as will the local environment. Moreover, in public services there is often a complex interaction of cause and effect. In social care a whole range of agencies, social security, the general practitioner, the National Health Service, and the housing service must interact to provide effective service. The measurement of performance in such cases raises the problem of assessing the relative contribution of the members of a team, especially where there may be different criteria for judgment within individual services. The educational organization poses the same problem, and the difficulties of assigning blame for failure are enhanced by the findings of various studies of school performance, emphasizing the importance of the overall school ethos and culture (Mortimore *et al*, 1988).

The Time Dimension

Measurement of performance must take account of the time dimension. In some cases it is fairly straightforward to measure the quality of a product as soon as it is produced. In other cases it will be very difficult to make a judgment of the success of activity until long after it has been carried out. An analogous problem is raised by the distinction between search goods and experience goods (Nelson, 1970). The former are goods which it is possible to assess before use, the latter are those which can only be assessed as or after we experience them. Services,

Measuring Quality

which are often used as they are produced, are particularly likely to be experience goods. A further category is the credence good, where it is difficult or impossible to measure quality either before or after the event, but the user must simply trust that they are getting a good service. Education has aspects of credence good if only because it is difficult to assess the results of the service in anything other than the long term. The process of performance measurement is likely to be difficult for experience and credence goods.

The Value of Ambiguity

The rationalistic world of performance measurement is concerned to reduce the degree of ambiguity faced by citizens, and by the managers of public service. Unambiguous performance measurement makes management at a distance, and control without contact, possible. It might seem that it would be for the best if we could measure everything and there was no room for argument. But we should not underestimate the value of ambiguity. In anything other than the most completely closed systems, there will always be unpredictable changes and developments. In such circumstances, existing patterns of behaviour are likely to be inappropriate, and there is a need to be able to be responsive while retaining stability. This requires a mixture of rigidity and flexibility, for adaptation at one level is made possible by rigidity at another. The information systems of complex organizations will consist not only of the hard facts of performance that may be measurable, but of stabilizing rules, and of a language that allows communication and adaptation.

Systems in which everything is measured are also likely to be systems in which there is a reduction in learning, especially learning through mistakes. A system of specified services, defined standards, and measured performance is likely to be one in which experimentation and risk are likely to be avoided.

The development of performance measurement often leads to a misleading view of the degree of precision which is possible. In systems of any size there are bound to be a large number of aspects of performance that can be measured and many different ways in which they can be measured. Decisions need to be made not only about which measures are to be used but how measures are to be combined. This is a problem that is well known in the failed planning systems of Eastern Europe and the Soviet Union. Nove (1983) has outlined the implications of the multiplicity of performance measures:

Quality, Surveillance and Performance Measurement

> The question of evaluating efficiency leads to the problem, familiar to most students of the Soviet economy, of success indicators. Plan instructions have to be expressed units of measurement: tonnes, square metres, millions of roubles, thousands of pairs and so on. In any instance where there is a product mix, or different types of dimensions, plan indicators must be aggregated ... But an order aggregated (for example, in tonne-kilometres) incites the recipient to act in a particular way. If the measure is tonnes, this rewards weight and penalises economy of materials. If the measure is gross-value in roubles there is a benefit to be derived from making expensive goods, using expensive materials. Tonne-kilometres incite transport undertakings to carry heavy goods over long distances ... (p. 73)

Similar results are likely in the public service unless it is possible to develop unambiguous measures of performance that are not aggregated. Experience suggests that unambiguous single measures are unlikely and that there will be a need to consider how to gauge measures against each other or combine them. The sort of complex measures that are likely to be developed, for example the quality adjusted life year (QALY), developed by health analysts, are open to such manipulation, and also raise deep philosophical and ethical questions. Unambiguous measures are likely to be available only for the simplest of services. Even in the private sector, where the common dimension of money is more easily available, it is difficult to measure performance where quality is involved. The more formal and standardized a system, the more difficult it is to change it in response to changing needs and patterns of service. Systems of measurement of service performance will reflect particular understanding of the nature and purposes of those services. Preston (1992), for example, shows the way that accounting systems in the health sector have had to change to reflect different understandings of the service. Formal measurement systems are likely to impede development the less they are congruent with need and the less they reflect changing circumstances. The public sector is perhaps even more prey to the dangers of the persistence of organizational measurement systems that have outlived their effectiveness and prevent effective adaptation.

Trust and Audit

The development of the public services in the post-war period was associated with a belief in the need for professionals and a trust in their judgments. In a complex world it is inevitable that we take many things on trust, otherwise our lives would be impossible as they became overburdened with the need to make decisions at every turn. The more we can take on trust, the more we can save our energies for what, for us, are the significant matters. Development and complexity bring with them the need to increase the degree to which we trust people with whom we have little contact. The wider is our network of contacts and the more fragmented our relationships, the more we have to trust that others with whom we interact will be able and willing to carry out their roles. The less we trust people the more we are forced to engage in surveillance, which is likely to be significantly more expensive than developing the bases on which we can rationally trust others. What is happening in the public service, and perhaps more generally, is that we are moving away from a system of extensive trust in a wide range of others to intensive trust in a new set of professionals in surveillance.

The growth of the new profession is apparent in the development of a large number of inspectorates and auditing and inspection processes over the last decade. The most important of these is the Audit Commission, responsible for far more than purely regulatory audit, having a wide-ranging brief to examine management practices. The Commission's brief has lately been extended to include the National Health Service. The Audit Commission has had a major impact on the activities of local government over the last ten years, and that influence has not been limited to management questions but has had significant policy impacts. The Commission has now been charged with developing the system of performance measurement for local government that is required as a result of the Citizen's Charter. Other new inspectorates include those for social services. Many of the long-standing inspectorates, such as that for police or fire have become more influential. The new 'marketized' education inspectorate is to operate in a way that is surveillance-oriented, rather than concerned with effective service development. It is part of the development of what Henkel (1991) has called the evaluative state.

The result is that problems of professional management and control tend to become reconstrued as problems of inspection. This can be seen in the reaction to failure. The reaction to the revelation of the use of 'pin-down' activities in some childrens' homes in Staffordshire, for example, was argued to be a need for more and better inspection, when the independent report on the affair showed that the problem was one of management failure and professional underdevelopment.

What is happening in public service management is akin to

the low trust dynamic described by Fox (1974) in the case of work organization. The low trust dynamic exists when outputs are strongly defined and highly rule bound. Any failure is taken to be the fault of the person who fails, and in consequence punishments are introduced, leading those working within the systems to try to evade being caught, leading to tighter rules and greater surveillance. In the high trust dynamic, by contrast, failure is not an occasion for blame but for help. Those facing difficulties are likely to cooperate in finding ways to improve performance if they are not punished for failure. The developments in the public sector seem to be focussed on the punishment-based rather than the developmental approach. Information is less valuable the later it comes and the less certain one can be of its accuracy. Account needs also to be taken of the extent to which the communication of information upward will lead to loss of content and accuracy. The distinction between measurement systems that create the possibility of hierarchical control and those that enable horizontal communication and adaptation is central. The less perfect the information, the less possible it is for authority to lay down appropriate patterns of action by command. It is also impossible to ensure that adaptation happens through command when the information on which to base command is available too slowly. In such circumstances it is necessary for those most directly involved to make judgments on the information that is immediately available to them.

Conclusion

Performance measurement systems must live with the potential contradiction between control and adaptation. The more complex the system with which they deal, the more the need for control must give way to the requirements of adaptation. The argument for the market, as made by theorists such as Hayek, is precisely that it is an information system that allows adaptation without planned control. There is an internal conflict in contemporary developments in public service management in the attempt to develop market and quasi-market mechanisms, while at the same time developing potentially rigid performance control systems. As Campbell (1982) argues:

> A healthy, evolving society needs as much variety of knowledge as possible, and this variety must be maintained constantly. (p. 261)

The danger of rigid performance information systems is that they prevent adaptation, change, and requisite variety.

It is necessary not only to develop measures of performance, but also the techniques by which they may effectively be used. As Hacking says of medical statistics in the late nineteenth century:

> There were, then, statistics galore, but few conclusive statistical inferences. They were tools of rhetoric, not science. For all the enthusiasm for numbers, they did not have the immediate effect that one would have expected. (Hacking, 1990, p. 85)

The use of statistics in the current debates about AIDS shows that this problem is still with us.

The present stage of development in the measurement of the performance of the public service is one of facts and statistics, but little technique. The conclusions that we derive from measures will depend upon the structures that we impose upon the data and the way in which we analyze it. For example, different modes of analysis will be appropriate to data which is characterized by relationships of implication or weak connectedness, where there is a probability of a relationship, rather than a necessary connection, and different results will follow than in cases of logical implication. We need not only measures of performance but the technology with which they can be used effectively.

The Citizen's Charter movement is concerned to shift power from the provider to the user, the citizen, who is conceived as the consumer of public services. Information on the nature and performance of the public services is central to the effective development of the intentions behind the Charter. I have tried to show, in this chapter, that the effective development of performance measurement and management in the public service must recognise the complexity of the problem. The production of crude facts will do little to help us in the search for improvement of the public service.

References

AUDIT COMMISSION (1992) *Developing Local Authority Housing Strategies*, London, HMSO.
CAMPBELL, J. (1982) *Grammatical Man: Information, Entropy, Language and Life*, Harmondsworth, Penguin.
CARTER, N. (1989) 'Performance indicators: "Backseat Driving" or "Hands Off" Control?', *Policy and Politics*, **17**, 2, pp. 131–8.

CARTER, N., KLEIN, R. and DAY, P. (1992) *How Organisations Measure Success: The Use of Performance Indicators in Government*, London, Routledge.

CULYER, A.J. and POSNETT, J. (1990) 'Hospital behaviour and competition' in CULYER, A.J., MAYNARD, A. and POSNETT, J. (Eds) *Competition in Health Care: Reforming the NHS*, London, Macmillan.

DEATON, A. and MUELLBAKER, B. (1980) *Economics and Consumer Behaviour*, Cambridge, Cambridge University Press.

DEPARTMENT OF HEALTH AND SOCIAL SECURITY (1983) *NHS Management Enquiry*, London, DHSS.

DINGWALL, R. and FENN, P. (1987) '"A respectable profession"? Sociological and economic perspectives on the regulation of professional services', *International Review of Law and Economics*, **7**, pp. 51–64.

FLYNN, R. (1992) *Structures of Control in Health Management*, London, Routledge.

FOX, A. (1974) *Beyond Contract: Work, Power and Trust Relations*, London, Faber and Faber.

FULTON, LORD (1968) *The Civil Service: Report of the Committee*, London, HMSO.

HACKING, I. (1990) *The Taming of Chance*, Cambridge, Cambridge University Press.

HENKEL, M. (1991) *Government, Evaluation and Change*, London, Jessica Kingsley.

HIRSCHMAN, A.O. (1970) *Exit, Voice and Loyalty*, Cambridge, MA, Harvard University Press.

KENNEY, R. and KLEIN, B. (1983) 'The economics of block booking', *Journal of Law and Economics*, **26**, pp. 497–540.

KOTLER, P. (1988) *Marketing Management: Analysis, Planning, Implementation and Control*, London, Macmillan.

MILLER, D. (1990) *The Icarus Paradox: How Exceptional Companies Bring About Their Own Downfall*, New York, Harper Collins.

MORTIMORE, P., SAMMONS, P., STOLL, L., LEWIS, D. and ECOB, R. (1988) *School Matters: The Junior Years*, Wells, Open Books.

NELSON, P. (1970) 'Information and consumer behaviour', *Journal of Political Economy*, **78**, pp. 729–54.

NORMANN, R. (1985) *Service Management: Strategy and Leadership in Service Businesses*, Chichester, Wiley.

NOVE, A. (1983) *The Economics of Feasible Socialism*, London, George Allen and Unwin.

PETERS, T.J. and WATERMAN, R.H. (1982) *In Search of Excellence*, New York, Harper and Row.

PRESTON, A.M. (1992) 'The birth of clinical accounting: A study of the emergence and transformation of discourses on costs and practices of accounting in US hospitals', *Accounting, Organization and Society*, **17**, 1, pp. 63–100.

PRIME MINISTER (1991) *The Citizen's Charter*, London, HMSO.

ROSS, S. (1973) 'The economic theory of agency: The principal's problem', *American Economic Review*, **63**, pp. 134–9.

WILLIAMS, B. (1985) *Ethics and the Limits of Philosophy*, London, Fontana.
WILSON, J.A. (1980) 'Adaptation to uncertainty and small numbers exchange: The New England fresh fish market', *Bell Journal of Economics*, **11**, 2, pp. 491–504.

Chapter 6

Performance Indicators: Flourish or Perish?

John Gray and Brian Wilcox

Introduction

Interest in performance indicators, and optimism about their potential, probably reached a peak amongst English LEAs in the late eighties. In the wake of the Education Reform Act the case for their introduction was made in several influential reports including one by a prestigious accountancy firm which had been asked to explore the local management of schools (Coopers and Lybrand, 1988) and another by the Audit Commission, the local authority 'watch-dog' (Audit Commission, 1989). Performance indicators would become, it was argued, one of the key mechanisms through which the monitoring and accountability of schools would be assured. The time seemed particularly propitious for their development and imaginative use within the school system.

The case for the introduction of performance indicators flows from the model of the school which is implicit in government educational policy of recent years. This seeks to describe schools in terms which refer directly to their 'performance' or 'effectiveness'. Such terms are applied to the achievements of the school, and especially those associated with the pupils. Pupil achievements are expressed most frequently as the knowledge, skills, characteristics and specific accomplishments acquired by individuals (often assessed in the form of examination results, test scores or behavioural measures); these are then aggregated into appropriate indicators of a statistical nature. The use of such indicators reinforces the popular tendency to see standards, targets and performance as unproblematic entities, 'out-there', measurable and (in the popular sense of the word) 'objective'. The fact that they are essentially abstractions, which have been socially-constructed and which arise from attempts to make sense of some parts of the complex realities called 'schools', is often forgotten.

Two or three years later it is clear that progress on the development of performance indicators has been slow and, at least in terms of the aspirations of enthusiasts, somewhat disappointing. They do not appear, as yet, to have become influential tools for management or evaluation purposes. The view of one LEA chief adviser we interviewed in early 1992 is not untypical. 'We set up a working group in 1988/89. There has been a lot of ink spilt on performance indicators since then and I don't know that we're much further forward.'

Why is it then that performance indicators have still to live up to their promise? What problems have to be surmounted before relevant and useful ones can be developed? These and related questions are considered below in the context of some recent initiatives.

Brainstorming the Agenda

Towards the end of 1989 Mrs. Rumbold, an Education Minister at that time, presented a long-awaited list of performance indicators for schools at a conference of the Industrial Society. This list, referred to as an *'aide-mémoire'* (DES, 1989), was one of the major outcomes of a year-long study involving some eight LEAs and some forty of their schools.

In introducing the list the Minister argued that it was intended to take debates about schools' effectiveness beyond merely looking at examination results. She is quoted as saying that: 'It is our job to make sure that parents recognize that there are other things going on in schools to prepare pupils for the world of work and life after school'; and later on that: 'The more we put across the fact that performance indicators go a lot further than exam results — important though they are — the better we shall be'. Each school was to be urged to decide on 'a relatively small range of indicators for judging whether it is achieving its goals' (Rumbold, 1989).

In practice any other advice about how to use the *'aide-mémoire'* would have been implausible. The various working groups had produced a dauntingly long list of items (fifty in all) many of which had been sub-divided into several parts. The items listed were also very heterogeneous. Some were expressed in specific and explicitly-quantifiable forms such as: 'the overall pupil-teacher ratio' (item 4) and 'the percentages of (year 11) pupils who continued into the sixth-form or entered sixth-form/tertiary college' (item 28). Others consisted of descriptive statements or questions such as: 'organization of the curriculum' (item 6) or 'School's objectives for community links? Are these being achieved? How does the school assess the local community's perception of its work? How does the school receive visitors?' (item 20).

Performance Indicators: Flourish or Perish?

Closer analysis of the items on the list reveals that twenty were descriptive whilst only twelve could be regarded as explicitly quantifiable. Another eleven could be regarded as implicitly quantifiable in cases where the quantifying categories were given in general rather than specific terms. Examples would include 'socioeconomic factors affecting the pupil population such as incomes, housing and employment' (item 14). Of the remaining seven items, five were a mixture of descriptive and explicit/implicit quantitative statements and two were just questions requiring a simple yes/no answer; for example, 'Does the school have a delegated budget under an approved LMS scheme?' (item 13). Seven of the items had trend-style questions appended to them implying access to data or experiences across several years; an example would be the question: 'Are such incidents of internal vandalism increasing or decreasing?' (item 35).

Several other features of the list are worthy of comment. First, its length was justified on the grounds that it provided a comprehensive set of indicators from which schools would be able to select a smaller sub-set for their own use. Potential users, however, would probably not find the list very helpful since, in most cases, they would be left with the difficult task of translating general descriptive statements into more specific and useable forms.

Second, the compilers of the *aide-mémoire* would probably justify the high proportion of descriptive statements on the grounds that they were 'keen to make it a priority to develop qualitative indicators (and . . . did not consider that (schools') success could be judged adequately by a few statistics' (Rumbold, 1989). Again, however, the difficult task of turning so-called qualitative indicators into useable categories is left to the individual user.

Third, perhaps the most striking feature of the *aide-mémoire* is its atheoretical nature. In launching it the Minister drew attention to the recently-published report by HM Inspectorate on effective school management (HMI, 1988). Whilst commending the HMI's report, however, it is not obvious how its criteria were related to the structure of the *aide-mémoire* which was simply organized under a number of conventional and minimalist headings: basic data; context; pupil achievement; pupil attitudes; and management.

Overall, then, the *aide-mémoire* seems to be a rather diffuse collection of statements representing, in the main, what heads, inspectors, LEA officers, teachers and DES officials collectively understood to be some of the features of 'effective schools'. It reflected many of the compromises that emerge when committees of educators sit down together to share views about what it is important to manage and assess.

Measuring Quality

It is easy to single out the DES project for comment because its products were amongst the most visible of the various attempts that were made at the turn of the decade to 'brainstorm' possible lists of performance indicators. It is important to stress, however, that similar comments and criticisms could have been applied just as easily to the lists and reports various other bodies produced around this time. These would include the so-called 'Blue Book' produced by a working party of LEA officials (CIPFA, 1988) and any number of locally-generated reports by heads and LEA officers.

Listing the multiple criteria by which schools *might* be judged seems to be endemic to the process of constructing performance indicators. It is a process which bears a notable resemblance to efforts in an earlier decade to construct lists of questions which schools might wish to ask themselves in the course of undertaking self-evaluative reviews (Clift *et al*, 1987).

Assembling Some Evidence

We have already hinted at some of the difficulties to be overcome in beginning to establish a framework for monitoring performance. Nonetheless, over a relatively short period of time there are indications that many LEAs had begun to make progress in putting something in place. As part of our recent PAQS (Programmes to Assess the Quality of Schooling) project we asked chief inspectors and advisers in England and Wales to tell us about the position in their own LEA in the year 1990/91. Did they have quantitative measures available to them to assist in forming judgments about schools? And, if they did, which ones.

The PAQS questionnaire presented respondents with a list of ten items and additional space to write in further items if they wished. Chief advisers and inspectors of ninety-nine of the 115 English and Welsh LEAs provided answers. Their responses in relation to secondary schools in their LEAs are listed in table 6.1.

Not surprisingly, measures of public examination results dominated the picture. Over three out of four reported that they had this measure available. It is of interest, given impending requirements for the publication of results, that one in four did not appear to be in this position during 1990/91. Roughly half the LEAs also had information available to them about pupils' post-16 destinations and attendance.

Amongst items relating to the contextual circumstances of individual schools, and the communities they served, two items of information emerged as particularly prominent — the incidence of free school

Table 6.1: Quantitative measures reported by LEAs as being available to them in 1990/91 to inform the judgment of secondary schools' performance

	% of all LEAs
Possible Outcome Measures	
Public Examination Results	78
Post-16 Destinations	55
Attendance	52
Exclusions	4
Possible Contextual Measures	
Incidence of Free School Meals	42
Incidence of Special Needs	44
Reading Tests	12
English Tests	9
Arithmetic/Mathematics	8
Verbal Reasoning Tests	8
Non-Verbal Reasoning Tests	5
Ethnic Backgrounds of Pupils	7
Other Measures of Pupil Attainment	5
Other Pupil Characteristics	8
Possible School Characteristics	
Staff	10
School	6
Finance/Resources	3
Parents/Community	3

Note: Based on ninety-nine responses out of 115 English and Welsh LEAs to the PAQS questionnaire.

meals and of special needs. In both cases just under half the LEAs had this information. It is likely that, in both cases, this information would have been needed for other administrative purposes within the authority and that ready availability was a by-product of these other demands. Information on other aspects of pupils' performance at the point of entry to secondary school or relating to their background circumstances was a good deal more limited. For each such item listed in table 6.1 only around one in ten LEAs claimed to have something available during 1990/91. Systematically-quantified information on other aspects of schools' characteristics also appeared to be in rather short supply.

It is perhaps important to stress that the position described in table 6.1 reflects the respondents' views of what was available for use; other information may have been to hand in other parts of their authorities. Nonetheless, the overall picture presented by the table is a patchy one. By the end of the eighties many LEAs (and perhaps a majority) do not appear to have had a systematically-organized database containing pertinent information of a quantitative kind available to them for ready use. Sometimes this was because they simply lacked the information; in other instances it was because the organizational conditions that would

Measuring Quality

have facilitated their construction had yet to materialize. At the time of writing it is a situation which many LEAs are taking further steps to redress.

The evidence in table 6.1 reveals a number of problems for those who are seeking to establish a national framework for judging schools' performances. As the position stood in 1990/91 it would not have been possible to construct (through the medium of LEAs' databases) a comprehensive national picture of schools' achievements for any outcome measure other than examination results — and even in this case it would have been an incomplete one. Some sense of the patterns relating to post-16 destinations and attendance would also have been possible but, in both cases, the picture would have been still more incomplete. In only around half the LEAs in the country could any analysis contextualizing schools' results have been attempted. In a rather small number of LEAs (and in some individual schools) a fuller picture would have been possible. By whatever standards one employs, however, the position revealed in table 6.1 offers no more than the rudimentary outlines of a possible national framework.

Turning Exam Results into a Convincing Account

The pressure on schools and LEAs to give a convincing account of their performance, as evinced by their pupils' examination results, has been on since the early eighties. Over the intervening period, however, the stakes have increased. What started as a requirement for schools to include details of their own results in the backs of their prospectuses has developed into a demand that LEAs publish the results of all schools in their localities in their local newspapers. The much-resisted spectre of 'league tables' has finally arrived.

There have been some refinements over this period in the nature of the information about pupils' performances which schools were expected to publish. In the latest regulations, certain kinds of comparative information about national and local averages, as well as performance in the previous year, must be included and some figures have to be calculated as a percentage of the pupils on the school roll rather than the number of candidates. But, essentially, these have been matters of refinement rather than fundamental reconstruction — when one is dealing with examination results the figures are somehow assumed to 'speak for themselves'.

In tandem with the debates about what exactly is to be published a fierce debate has been raging about what, if anything, it all appears to mean. In brief, can one legitimately infer anything from the examination results of the pupils about the performance of their schools? Do the figures, in practice, tell one any more about the school than what kinds of pupils it was in a position to attract in the first place? Knowing how pupils actually performed is an important part of the information one would require to make this judgment but few educators have thought it sufficient.

Although practitioners have drawn heavily on the findings of research on school effectiveness, research perspectives have been noticeably absent from most of the debates about performance indicators. There has been one exception to this general pattern. Attempts to contextualize schools' examination results have drawn heavily on statistical techniques adopted by researchers and have continued to develop in relation to them. In the early eighties various attempts were made to contextualize schools' results using information about the social background characteristics of their intakes (see Gray, 1981 for an early account). Interestingly, more recent developments in the underlying statistical theories have been taken up as understanding of the potential of so-called 'value-added' approaches has increased (Aitkin and Longford, 1986; Gray *et al*, 1986).

Most surprisingly of all, perhaps, certain LEAs have sought out researchers capable of undertaking analyses using the most sophisticated statistical techniques. In particular, there has been heightened interest in the potential of multi-level approaches and their application (see, for example, Nuttall *et al*, 1989; Gray *et al*, 1990). Indeed, we ourselves have collaborated with one LEA where such ideas have already been disseminated to headteachers and begun to inform their practice (for a fuller account see Hedger, 1992). In brief, analytical and statistical approaches which were, until recently, defeating leading statisticians and the largest computers have begun to become part of the evaluation armoury in a small number of LEAs.

Extending the Account

Whilst there is widespread agreement that schools' examination results could be important indicators of performance few LEAs seem to be happy with the idea that they are sufficient. Consequently, in one way or another, most have begun to develop their own 'criteria for judgment'.

'Criteria for judgment' have emerged in many LEAs as part of their programmes for monitoring and evaluating schools introduced in the wake of the 1988 Education Reform Act. Whilst they share some features in common with performance indicators, however, their development has often occurred alongside, and often separately, from them. A distinction needs to be maintained between the two although this is essentially a matter of degree. Performance indicators tend to be quantitative measures of organizational aspects, often characterized in input and output terms. In contrast, criteria are more specific, qualitative statements describing the processes which are assumed to mediate inputs and outputs.

The *Criteria for School Evaluation* developed by Suffolk LEA are a good example of the kind of approach LEAs have adopted (Suffolk LEA, 1990). These criteria are organized on an essentially hierarchical basis. A total of 183 'success criteria' are grouped under sixty-three criterial statements. These, in turn, are organized under eighteen broad statements about effectiveness in five key areas of the school's operation: school aims; the ethos of the school; curriculum organization and assessment; curriculum implementation; and management and administration.

An example may help to clarify the nature of the exercise:

> Resources and tasks are differentiated to take account of pupils' abilities and needs.

is one of three success criteria which fall under the broader criterion,

> The pace and scope of work provides a real and continuous challenge to pupils.

which, in turn, is one of six items related to the effectiveness statement,

> Learning activities are purposeful.

The latter, together with a further five statements, constitute the key area of 'curriculum implementation'.

There are at least three important questions that can be asked of such criterial lists. Why and how have they been produced? How are they used in practice? And in what ways do they relate to performance indicators?

The pressure to produce criterial lists has largely emerged, we suspect, from the perceived need to make inspection and external evaluation more credible and acceptable both to schools and other users. Credibility, in turn, has been linked with the requirements of 'objectivity'. In the words of the influential Audit Commission report,

'The observations on which reports to an institution are based should be made against pre-stated criteria of judgment' (Audit Commission, 1989, p. 18). Criteria have typically been made available to schools and, in some cases, developed in conjunction with them through the agency of working parties composed of teachers and LEA staff. In many LEAs this way of working has tended to be seen as an overt expression of the LEA's commitment to partnership with its schools.

The actual content of criterial lists has been influenced by at least three sources. The practices of HM Inspectorate have been particularly prominent. Traditionally HMI have not published their criteria for inspecting schools. However, as a result of increased interaction between HMI and LEA inspectorates in recent years, much of their practice has become fairly common knowledge and, at the time of writing, further developments are imminent. A second source has been generally agreed notions of so-called 'good practice'. Finally, claims are sometimes made that the choice of criteria has been influenced by research into school effectiveness. Research findings emphasizing the leadership role of the headteacher, for example, are sometimes reflected in such criteria as: 'The headteacher and senior staff maintain a clear, positive and consistent sense of direction; staff and pupils are motivated by the headteacher's personal interest, encouragement and concern; the headteacher gets directly involved in improvements, particularly in the early stages' (Salford LEA, 1991).

Rather little is known about how such criteria are used in the various kinds of reviews and evaluations commonly carried out in LEAs. Although a lot of effort has gone into the compilation of criteria, little seems to have been devoted to specifying exactly how these criteria should be used in observing school and classroom processes and constructing the notes and reports which inspectors subsequently make. In addition, few if any inspectorates, including HMI, have been able to offer evidence that their criteria are, in fact, applied consistently from occasion to occasion and from inspector to inspector (for a further discussion of this see Wilcox, 1992, pp. 191–6).

One method of using criteria is to combine them with rating scales. This strategy offers a means through which criteria can be developed into performance indicators. HMI have contributed more than most groups to developments in this respect, applying five-point scales to a variety of key areas of school and classroom life. The ratings are designed to accompany the descriptive and evaluative notes made by the inspectors and the scale is defined in terms of the retrievability value of the associated text. A rating of 1, therefore, corresponds to: 'generally good, or with some outstanding features; very useful for retrievers of good practice'. At the other end of the scale a rating of 5 indicates: 'many shortcomings, generally poor; very useful for retrievers for examples of bad conditions, unsound practice, etc' (HMI, 1988).

If separate ratings are made of similar aspects in a variety of circumstances these can then be aggregated into percentages falling into particular categories. HMI's ratings of schools' performance were summarized in the following terms, for example, in their Annual Report on the state of the nation's schooling:

> In the 18,000 lessons seen in over 2400 secondary schools work was satisfactory or better in 73 per cent of the lessons, including 31 per cent where it was good. (HMI, 1992, p. 16)

Similar kinds of evidence were in the process of being prepared for the annual reports of the Chief Inspector of the Inner London Education Authority, prior to its demise. Since that time a small number of other LEA inspectorates have also adopted variants of HMI's approach. In Wandsworth, for example, a system has been trialled in which features of particular lessons are observed and rated on a scale defined by three points: E (exemplary); A (acceptable); and D (requires further development). Lessons are rated in five major areas which are: planning; clarity of purpose; teaching approaches; pupil conduct and involvement; and evidence of learning. From these various pieces of information a summary score is then derived using a four-point scale on which a 1, for example, denotes an 'exemplary' rating on all five aspects of performance.

The combination of rating scales and criteria would appear to offer a promising method of generating performance indicators that goes beyond the easily measurable to embrace some aspects of the quality of educational experiences and provision. However, before indicators derived in this manner can be expected to become publicly credible, it is essential that inspectorates demonstrate that they can achieve acceptable levels of consistency. To date few seem to have accepted this particular challenge.

The Agenda for the 1990s

Will the 1990s see the coming of age of performance indicators or will they continue to languish as a specialist interest, having only a rather marginal effect on school management and planning? The position, in our view, is finely poised. Performance indicators could easily join the scrap-heap of 'good ideas'. If the momentum of earlier developments is to be sustained various steps will need to be taken fairly soon.

From the perspective of those whose job it is to report on (or provide information about) the quality of the nation's schooling there is a compelling logic to the development of performance indicators. How can a school be run effectively and efficiently, they ask, if the areas in which it is trying to perform are not known and evaluated systematically? And surely, if those involved in running a school have sorted out what it is they are trying to achieve and how to evaluate it, they stand a better chance of succeeding? From this perspective, the introduction of some kind of system of performance assessment seems to be an obvious next step in managing the development of the institution.

On the other hand, from the perspective of the practitioner, it seems to have been perfectly possible to run an institution without any elaborate system of performance indicators at all. Furthermore, although there is evidence in the literature that 'good schools' often know fairly precisely what their objectives are and whether they are achieving them (see, for example, Lightfoot, 1983), there is a noticeable dearth of evidence that they have actually been assisted in reaching their position by virtue of having (systems of) performance indicators in place. It is not difficult to see how the innovation can have come to be perceived, in many situations, as serving someone's interests — but not necessarily the school's!

The impetus for the introduction of performance indicators frequently stems from a particular view of how schools ought to be managed. Coleman and LaRocque (1990), in their study of Canadian school districts, report that 'careful monitoring of school performance (was) central to accountability, and a distinguishing characteristic of unusually effective school districts' (p. 95). But they also argue that for performance monitoring to become an accepted district practice, 'leaders must create and sustain some commitment to monitoring from educators, and particularly from school principals'. In many contexts creating this commitment has proved difficult. Based on a study of aspects of the American experience, for example, a group of HMI recently commented that: 'the approach, in principle, is to monitor the schools, present them with the performance data and then leave it to the principals, together with parents and general administrative guidance from the district, to take the school forward' (HMI, 1991, p. 22). They go on to note, however, that teachers' reactions 'were mixed. Most accepted and worked in the system without complaint ... (but) saw themselves as having something to lose and expressed a good deal of cynicism about the value of reporting and the time and effort that were involved'.

Few LEAs in this country would appear, to date, to have achieved the levels of commitment that are necessary. Whilst there are signs that British schools may be moving in similar directions to some of the North American ones, the differences between the two systems are more striking at the current time. The suspicion that performance indicators are something which is done to schools, rather than for or with them, remains.

There is a case to be made for schools themselves taking the initiative in developing measures. In his engagingly-titled book *Thriving on Chaos* Peters (1987) suggests that 'measuring what's important' should be a 'guiding premise' for any organization's development. There is one difference between his recommendations and those which have typically been implemented in educational organizations. In his view 'every manager should track no more than three to five variables which capture the essence of the business' (*ibid.*, p. 482). To date, however, most educational institutions have found themselves in this position by default rather than design.

Building on such approaches in the context of education Beare and colleagues (1989) argue that performance indicators are essential, if individual institutions are to answer questions about their relative 'excellence' and, simultaneously, to establish directions for their future development. But they also acknowledge that 'in education the primary criteria are more difficult to calculate than they are in a business firm and that, consequently, secondary criteria must be established relating to: process, patterns, output, organizational structures, and input'. Very little advice has been forthcoming, however, about how a school might set about establishing such measures, other than merely accepting those which others have made available; Hargreaves and Hopkins' (1991) account of how schools might set about establishing what they call 'success criteria', as part of their process of development planning, is a notable exception. And, in practice, Peters' advice about drastically limiting the numbers of measures seems to get ignored. In short, it is an exceptionally well-organized school that can move quickly towards the kind of coherence of purpose and practice that systems of performance indicators imply. In such situations performance indicators can easily come to be seen as unwelcome harbingers of changing regimes of accountability rather than as potential contributors to schools' development.

Stumbling Blocks and Challenges

It is already evident from our discussion that several of the steps that need to be taken are posing considerable problems. Whatever their promise, the introduction of performance indicators into British schools must rank amongst the most difficult in recent years. Several challenges need to be faced.

The first is the need to be clear what kinds of measures might actually count as performance indicators (and, by extension, which might not) and to concentrate effort on some of the most important ones. As one of us has argued elsewhere, performance indicators should be first and foremost about *schools'* performance (Gray and Jesson, 1991). Failure to be explicit in this respect can rapidly lead to conceptually-sloppy collections of broad evaluative and descriptive statements which do little to guide the policy and planning processes of an institution.

As Scheerens (1990) has argued, performance indicators should allow value judgments to be made about key aspects of the functioning of educational systems in some quantifiable form; they should speak, in brief, to issues of quality. Many of the measures which have been put forward to date as possible performance indicators fail on one of these two counts: they are either not obviously about the school's contribution to pupils' development or they do not lend themselves readily to assessment. Measures which are of a sufficiently high quality to do justice to schools' efforts usually require time to develop; what is available off-the-shelf is rarely immediately suitable. As Murnane (1987) has shown, in a comparison of indicators available to economists and educators, many of these problems are generic to the development of all indicator systems and not just those in education.

Second, there is an urgent need to develop a wider range of measures. There is widespread agreement that exam and test results are not sufficient to do justice to schools' efforts. With the introduction of testing at all four key stages of the National Curriculum, however, schools will probably be deluged by information pertaining to their pupils' cognitive performances. Some effort will need to be devoted to constructing further measures to place alongside these kinds of outcomes, if broader views about the nature and purposes of education are to be given credence. Indeed, one of us has suggested that there are just three priorities: the continuing development of: (i) more sophisticated approaches to the analysis of pupils' academic progress should be complemented by something relating (ii) to pupils' satisfaction with their educational experiences; and (iii) to aspects of pupil-teacher relationships (Gray, 1990).

The government itself is committed to introducing more information about pupils' attendance at school and their subsequent post-16 destinations. Important as these measures are, however, they still represent a rather limited view of what schools are about. Small numbers of LEAs and their schools are currently engaged in trying to extend the range of possibilities. Such initiatives are at the stage where they need to be nurtured (for a slightly fuller account see Gray, Jesson and Sime, 1991). A fraction of the energy which has been devoted to the analysis of examination results could yield substantial results, especially where attempts are made to combine different kinds of information about pupils' attitudes and responses (Fitz-Gibbon, 1992).

The third area requiring development is perhaps the most controversial. Given the complexity and variety of potential educational outcomes, it is unlikely that the quality of schools can ever be adequately described in pupil performance terms alone. Consequently there has been considerable interest amongst LEA inspectors in so-called process indicators which speak to the ways in which human and other resources in schools are organized and deployed to realize educational aims. Such indicators are seen as important for two main reasons. They may provide some kind of basis for interpreting or explaining the levels of pupil performance revealed by existing indicators. Differences in attainments in different subject areas may, for example, be accounted for by differences in the quality of the teaching/learning resources available. They may also act as a kind of guarantor that wider educational aims, not easily assessed by testing pupils, are likely to be realized. Regular opportunities for pupils to discuss contemporary issues, for example, may lend some support to the view that certain kinds of intellectual independence are being fostered.

By concentrating on pupil outcomes some would argue that the need to explore process indicators is obviated. Schools should be left to their own devices as regards the means by which they achieve their outcomes. Certainly there is a danger that by entering into this field one is inviting the construction of increasingly lengthy lists of factors which collectively amount to a form of 'good school' blueprint. On the other hand, to ignore such measures completely gives hostage to potentially dull, uninspiring, instrumentally-oriented strategies.

A number of researchers and practitioners have argued that research on school effectiveness provides (or could provide) some important pointers; very few, however, have to date attempted anything very systematic by way of identifying what these might be. A notable exception is a review conducted by Oakes (1989) in which three areas are targeted as good candidates for indicator development.

Performance Indicators: Flourish or Perish?

She too generates lengthy lists but also argues that a 'barebones' version can be sustained. Its components are as follows:

(i) 'Access to knowledge': the extent to which schools provide opportunities for pupils to learn domains of knowledge and skills.
(ii) 'Press for achievement': the institutional strategies the school exerts in order to motivate and sustain its pupils.
(iii) 'Professional teaching conditions': the circumstances that can empower teachers and others as they attempt to implement educational programmes.

Oakes claims, on the basis of her reading of the research literature, that the quality of teaching and learning in a school is likely to be a direct function of these three enabling conditions. Each is, of course, composed of a number of individual school features and characteristics. Consequently, when her conceptual framework is laid out it resembles, superficially at least, the less rigorously-derived criteria lists developed in many LEAs. Although Oakes does not make this point, her 'conditions' could be operationalized as indicators using the kind of rating techniques we have described earlier.

Some of the challenges we have outlined may be met through the implementation of recent government policy initiatives. For example, the government appears somewhat more aware of the limitations of simple 'league table' approaches to school performance and more favourably disposed to attempts to complement them with 'value added' interpretations:

> As age groups of pupils move from one key stage of the National Curriculum to the next and beyond, it will be possible to compare the results they achieve and so measure more effectively the value added to pupils' education by individual schools. (DFE, 1992a, p. 16)

This commitment to added value is further reinforced by the procedures for dealing with schools at risk of failing as outlined in the framework for the new inspection arrangements of schools (DFE, 1992b). One of the factors to be considered in designating such schools will be the level of examination results attained in relation to those of comparable schools.

The new inspection arrangements may also play a crucial role in the more general development and use of performance indicators. Registered inspectors will be required to demonstrate, *inter alia*, that their judgments 'are rooted in a substantial evidence base and informed by specified quantitative indicators' (*ibid.*, p. 2). A basic core of eleven areas, which are termed indicators, is initially envisaged and broadened to include several concerned with financial performance. Whether these go far enough to meet the concerns we have outlined is questionable.

The inspection framework is also potentially noteworthy in another respect. Although not explicitly based on effectiveness research, the framework sets out a structure for schools organized under a limited number of broad factors: quality of teaching; assessment; recording and reporting; quality and range of the curriculum; management and planning; organization and administration; resources and their management; pupils' support and guidance; liaison and community links. Each of these factors will form headings for major sections in the reports which the new independent inspection teams will write on the schools they inspect. In addition, it is possible that these factors, or ones very much like them, will form the basis for a number of key process indicators. This is because the new inspection reports will also be the main source from which judgments about the school system nationally will be made. This is likely to be the case since HMI will be both a smaller force than formerly and largely concerned with monitoring the inspection activities of the independent teams rather than carrying out inspections themselves.

If the national judgments of the kind offered in the past by HMI are to continue, then they will arise from an aggregation of the ratings made by the new inspection teams. If such indicators are to achieve public credibility it will be necessary to demonstrate that the assessments on which they are based can be made consistently both within and across different inspection teams. Whether or not the training programmes for inspectors and the periodic consistency checks carried out by HMI will be able to guarantee this requirement remains to be seen.

Furthermore, will a reduced force of HMI and a loose network of independent inspection teams have the time and commitment to establish the organizational structures necessary to sustain a nationwide system of performance indicators — particularly in a future where the role and influence of LEAs may be dramatically reduced?

The development of performance indicators beyond their present relatively limited level of use is therefore at the present time a moot point.

Acknowledgments

Much of the work reported in this chapter was undertaken as part of the PAQS research project in the QQSE Research Group in the Division of Education at the University of Sheffield. The project is exploring 'LEA Programmes to Assess the Quality of Schooling'. We should particularly like to thank the Economic and Social Research Council for their support in relation to this research (ref. no. R000 23 3227) and the numerous LEA officers and teachers who have answered our questions.

References

AITKIN, M. and LONGFORD, N. (1986) 'Statistical issues in school effectiveness', *Journal of Royal Statistical Society*, Series A, **149**, pp. 1–42.
AUDIT COMMISSION (1989) *Assuring Quality in Education*, London, HMSO.
BEARE, H., CALDWELL, B.J. and MILLIKAN, R.H. (1989) *Creating an Excellent School: Some New Management Techniques*, London, Routledge.
CIPFA (1988) *Performance Indicators for Schools*, London, Chartered Institute of Public Finance and Accountancy.
CLIFT, P.S., NUTTALL, D.L. and McCORMICK, R. (1987) *Studies in School Self-Evaluation*, Lewes, Falmer Press.
COLEMAN, P. and LaROCQUE, L. (1990) *Struggling to be 'Good Enough': Adminstrative Practices and School District Ethos*, London, Falmer Press.
COOPERS AND LYBRAND (1988) *Local Management of Schools*, London, HMSO.
DEPARTMENT OF EDUCATION AND SCIENCE (1988) *Secondary Schools: An Appraisal by HMI*, London, HMSO.
DEPARTMENT OF EDUCATION AND SCIENCE (1989) *School Indicators for Internal Management*, London, Department of Education and Science.
DEPARTMENT FOR EDUCATION (1992a) *Choice and Diversity: A New Framework for Schools*, Cmnd 2021, London, HMSO.
DEPARTMENT FOR EDUCATION (1992b) *Framework for the Inspection of Schools*, paper for consultation, London, HMSO.
FITZ-GIBBON, C.T. (1992) 'School effects at 'A' Level: Genesis of an information system?' in REYNOLDS, D. and CUTTANCE P. (Eds) *School Effectiveness: Research, Policy and Practice*, London, Cassell.
GRAY, J. (1981) 'A competitive edge: Examination results and the probable limits of secondary school effectiveness', *Educational Review*, **33**, 1, pp. 25–35.
GRAY, J. (1990) 'The quality of schooling: Frameworks for judgment', *British Journal of Educational Studies*, **38**, 3, pp. 204–23.
GRAY, J. and JESSON, D. (1991) 'The negotiation and construction of performance indicators', *Evaluation and Research in Education*, **4**, 2, pp. 93–108.

GRAY, J., JESSON, D. and JONES, B. (1986) 'The search for a fairer way of comparing schools' examination results', *Research Papers in Education*, **1**, 2, pp. 91–122.

GRAY, J., JESSON, D. and SIME, N. (1990) 'Estimating differences in the examination performances of secondary schools in six LEAs: A multi-level approach to school effectiveness', *Oxford Review of Education*, **16**, 2, pp. 137–58.

GRAY, J., JESSON, D. and SIME, N. (1991) 'Developing LEA frameworks for monitoring and evaluation from research on school effectiveness: problems, progress and possibilities' in RIDDELL, S. and BROWN, S. (Eds) *School Effectiveness Research: Its Messages for School Improvement*, Edinburgh, HMSO.

HARGREAVES, D.H. and HOPKINS, D. (1991) *The Empowered School*, London, Cassell.

HEDGER, K. (1992) 'Seen it; been there; done it: The analysis of GCSE examination results in Shropshire', *Management in Education*, **6**, 1, pp. 29–33.

HER MAJESTY'S INSPECTORATE (1988) 'Rating scales and HMI exercises', *Working Instruction 27/87*, London, DES.

HER MAJESTY'S INSPECTORATE (1991) *Aspects of Education in the USA: Indicators in Educational Monitoring*, London, HMSO.

HER MAJESTY'S INSPECTORATE (1992) *Education in England 1990–91: The Annual Report of HM Senior Chief Inspector of Schools*, London, Department of Education and Science.

LIGHTFOOT, S.L. (1983) *The Good High School: Portraits of Character and Culture*, New York, Basic Books.

MURNANE, R.J. (1987) 'Improving education indicators and economic indicators: The same problems?', *Educational Evaluation and Policy Analysis*, **9**, 2, pp. 101–16.

NUTTALL, D., GOLDSTEIN, H., PROSSER, R. and RASBASH, J. (1989) 'Differential school effectiveness', *International Journal of Educational Research*, **13**, 7, pp. 769–76.

OAKES, J. (1989) 'School context and organization', in SHAVELSON, R.J., McDONNELL, L.M. and OAKES, J. (Eds) (1989) *Indicators for Monitoring Mathematics and Science Education*, Santa Monica, CA, Rand Corporation, pp. 40–65.

PETERS, T. (1987) *Thriving on Chaos: Handbook for a Management Revolution*, London, Pan Books.

RUMBOLD, A. (1989) *Times Educational Supplement*, 8 December.

SALFORD LEA (1991) 'Management generic pointers' (draft), *Reporting Practice*, Salford, Education Department.

SCHEERENS, J. (1990) 'School effectiveness research and the development of process indicators of school functioning', *School Effectiveness and School Improvement*, **1**, 1, pp. 61–80.

SUFFOLK LEA (1990) *Suffolk Criteria for School Evaluation*, Ipswich, Suffolk County Council.

WILCOX, B. (1992) *Time-Constrained Evaluation: A Practical Approach for LEAs and Schools*, London, Routledge.

Chapter 7

Following the Education Indicators Trail in the Pursuit of Quality

Kathryn A. Riley

This chapter examines the broader context for the development of performance indicators in the United Kingdom. It probes the relationship between the development of education indicators and methods of assessing institutional effectiveness, examining the current dilemmas facing schools and institutions in developing education indicators. The chapter also explores how the education context for the measurement of performance has become defined by the framework for inspection established by the 1992 Education (Schools) Act and by the 1993 Education Act and examines whether there is still scope for local interpretation.

Performance Indicators: Dials or Tin-openers?

The United Kingdom agenda for the development of performance indicators has been influenced by national government concerns about value for money. Public sector bodies, such as health or education authorities, were to be scrutinized to establish their efficiency. The model adopted to assess effectiveness was largely a Treasury-led throughput model, aimed at tracking information at different stages in a system and at providing clear and unambiguous measures of input and output.[1]

This throughput model has been described as equating performance indicators to 'dials' — similar to those on the dashboard of a car — which would provide clear and unambiguous measures of output. Measures of performance are instead, more contestable notions, influenced by a complex range of factors and are perhaps more aptly described as 'tin openers' which open up a 'can of worms' and lead to further examination and enquiry (Carter, 1989).

Recent United States proposals for a national education indicators information system (described in chapter 3), similarly reject the 'educational inputs — educational processes — educational outputs' model as being flawed. The authors of the American proposals argue that such a model limits attempts at school improvement, by encouraging the view that education systems take raw material (students), process them and produce products (*Education Counts*, 1991).

Within the United Kingdom debate on education indicators, the dials' analysis has mainly held sway at a national level, although there have been attempts to develop a broader perspective. In 1989, for example, the Department of Education and Science (DES), undertook a pilot project with eight local authorities to develop national criteria for performance measurement. The project's objectives were two-fold: to increase accountability of schools to parents and governors; and to develop objective indicators which would be capable of 'national aggregation'. The outcome of the project was limited, however, to the publication of an *aide-mémoire* of some fifty items, entitled *School Indicators for Internal Management* which offered neither a clear managerial approach nor a focus on accountability and as such added little to the debate (DES, 1989a; Riley, 1990).

Apart from this largely unsuccessful foray, the 'dials' perspective has increasingly been favoured by central government and has been used to sustain a critique of local government. Central government has asserted that local government has not made the improvement of quality a major objective and has thus failed to deliver a high quality education service. The government has therefore largely bypassed LEAs and sought to call schools directly to account for their performance, by making such indicators as examination performance a central form of evaluation.

Thus the 1992 Education (Schools) Act requires schools to publish information about examination and performance on national test scores, together with information about truancy rates and destinations of school leavers.[2] This information provides some indication of the healthiness of the school system but by no means the whole picture. The danger is that the indicators introduced by central government (which reflect only a limited education agenda), will increasingly define it.

Developing Education Indicator Systems

Objectives and Strategies

Education indicators are part of the search for information about educational outcomes and part of an evaluative system. The belief which underpins the development of education indicator systems is that the provision of information will optimize the conditions for improvement. Education indicator systems are designed to strengthen monitoring and evaluation and provide accurate and comprehensive information as a basis for effective policy-making and improved educational outcomes.

The conceptual and technical complexities of developing effective indicators systems are considerable and have been the subject of comprehensive study. Nuttall (1991 and chapter 2), for example, has suggested that policy, practical and technical issues influence the creation of indicators but that these may come into conflict with each other. A policy decision, for example, to create an education indicators system which attempted to incorporate different value systems would require a complex range of information, raising both technical and cost issues.

Debate has also focused on the characteristics which constitute effective education indicator systems. Carter (1991), for example, has argued that for systems to be effective they need to centre on institutional objectives and capabilities. Effective systems are typified by data sets which:

— are designed by the organization itself;
— provide information quickly on a relatively small range of indicators;
— and are linked to organizational objectives.

Carter has also suggested that the task of designing an indicators system would be easier if both quality and consumer satisfaction were regarded as processes: ways in which the service was delivered. Quality would therefore be a product of routine activities in the organization being carried out competently.

Approaches to the Development of Indicators

At the local level the development of education indicators has had a chequered career. In 1989, HMI reported that only a minority of LEAs were systematically interpreting the information which they had about examination performance (DES, 1989b). Few LEAs had integrated information systems effectively, or linked them to inspection, or been clear enough about the purposes of inspection. Partnership, between teachers, parents, students and governors had frequently been sketchy and characterized by one-way communication. Attempts to introduce indicator systems had tended to be *ad hoc* and top down but there had also been professional resistance to the use of indicators as measures of public accountability and few attempts to develop indicator systems which mapped the interrelationship between the experiences of users (students) and producers (teachers), or which integrated equality issues.

This picture has now shifted significantly, as will be described later in the chapter, and more formalized approaches are and have been developed. A study carried out by the author in 1991, for example, which examined how ten local authorities had developed education indicator systems, found substantial evidence of a trend towards the development of effective indicator systems (Riley, 1992).

The study identified two main approaches to the development of education indicators which were categorized as inspection and self-evaluation. The two approaches reflected different traditions and perspectives on inspection and differing assumptions about the relationship between the local education authority and schools.

The inspection approach focused on the importance of creating audited information to inform inspection and on the development of shared and negotiated agreements with schools about inspectorate judgments. The focus on public accountability brought about the Education Reform Act 1988 highlighted the need for local education authorities to develop a comprehensive review process for all schools. Education indicators were part of that process.

The approach relied on external judgments made by the Inspectorate and on the collection of high quality data from schools such as: examination results, pupil exclusions, post-school destinations, attendance data — the latter, in particular, being seen to have a major influence on academic achievement. The provision of such information was also intended to serve as a management tool for schools — for professional, resource and organizational decision-making.

The emphasis on accountability of schools for their performance and on the contribution of support services such as the Inspectorate to the enhancement of that performance, provided the basis for a new relationship between schools and the Inspectorate. This new relationship relied on the drawing up of agreed criteria for inspection and the development of ways of sharing that criteria and Inspectorate judgments with schools. It also identified the need, although not always the strategy, to help those involved take action. The approach was summed up in the following terms by one LEA inspector:

> The fundamental principle of our approach is that headteachers and governors must have a view of what is quality. The inspectors' role is to authenticate that view. It is essential that schools

have an objective evaluation of quality ... For this you need procedures and competency.

The self-evaluation approach drew heavily on the literature on school effectiveness and school improvement. It highlighted the school's own internal capacity to engage in review and reflection and through this, improve the quality of the education service offered.

The approach was one which emphasized the development of education indicators as a process rather than an outcome — a formative dialogue between schools and the external advisers or inspectors. The indicators generated by the school were usually qualitative rather than quantitative but were aimed at being capable of observation. The indicators developed were intended to provide the framework for action over a period of time and a mechanism through which schools could demonstrate that they had achieved their stated goals.

The strength of the self-evaluation approach was that it focused on the school as the primary actor. Its weakness lay in the assumption that a school could always identify its own limitations and take action to remedy them: parochialism could limit individual schools expectations about pupils achievement. One headteacher described the approach in the following terms:

> The LEA is managing a franchise. Schools market that franchise. Each school has its own character but it shares communal objectives which make it part of the club. The underpinning element for all schools is to make them healthy and buoyant ... If local education authorities think towards that end, it will provide them with their framework.

Designing a System at the Local Level

Developing an effective education indicator system requires an exploration of issues at a range of levels and an analysis of the relative purposes of indicators for schools, LEAs and central government. Clarity is needed about the information base; the sources of evaluation; the purposes and uses of evaluation at each level of the system.

At the *classroom level* there is a need to explore the relevance of classroom instruments and the relationship between indicators and inspection. At the *school level*, the focus needs to be on the relationship between indicators and school development plans. Underpinning all of this is the issue of ownership by all the staff within the organization.

The *LEA* can play a part in the process of developing this system, (particularly if it wants to support outcomes),

— by working with stakeholders to articulate the purposes of the system;
— by developing appropriate instruments and instilling confidence in the system;
— by virtue of its ability to compare and contrast, and provide schools with models which will enable them to reflect on their own performance;
— by linking the internal processes of self-review with those of external audit and validation;
— and by developing the concept of value added.

The systems which schools and LEAs design need to take into account existing information systems; reflect organizational purposes and local objectives; and present information in user friendly ways. At the heart of the design issue, however, rests such fundamental questions:

• who chooses the indicators?
• what are their purposes?

Indicators could be selected from a technical or managerial perspective; from a policy perspective; or from a more pluralistic accountability perspective. Each perspective is value laden and in this, as in other areas, the LEA's role is to mediate those complex interests; manage the conflict inherent in such a value laden activity; and provide a bridge between local purposes and national goals.

For LEAs, the development of an effective education indicator system provides the opportunity to the legitimate professional task of supporting the process of teaching and learning, with external validation of these outcomes and their translation into a more public arena. Such an approach can only be achieved, however, in partnership with schools and is also dependent on the willingness and ability of the LEA itself to open its own services to similar scrutiny and review.

LEAs and school face the complex and difficult task of integrating external inspection with internal self-evaluation. It is a task of consolidation, of linking the formative dialogue essential if schools are to engage in review and reflection, with that of external validation. It is also the task of creating the framework through which schools and the local education authorities which support them, become more publicly accountable for the quality of the education experience offered to children.

The development of education indicator systems presents a major challenge for schools and LEAs. *An effective indicators system which accommodated both managerial concerns about improvement and public concerns about progress could provide a powerful shift in the relationship between parents and school.* Such a pluralist approach could provide a link between narrow market definitions of performance and a broader model which encompasses the value added by schools and by the LEA through the work of both officers and members. It is also an approach which could enable the LEA to develop an advocacy role in respect of users of the service.

If such local systems were to be developed, they would be in marked contrast to the current UK national framework for education indicators which focus on limited skills and provide only a partial reflection of achievement but which are increasingly becoming the major goals of schooling. The national framework represents a limited interpretation of educational achievement and offers to the public a narrow analysis of what is happening in the education system.

Tackling Indicators on the Ground

Over the last few years, there has been a strong push from LEAs to develop evaluative frameworks to monitor academic progress and interpret school examination results (Gray *et al*, 1991; Gray and Wilcox, chapter 6). The experience of those schools and LEAs that have attempted to develop education indicators and integrate these into an evaluative system suggests that there are two important elements. The first is the establishment of a clear strategy about the process of developing indicators (including the principles and focus of action) and the second is clarity about values and purposes.

The process for the development of the indicators framework is a vital ingredient in developing an effective system. It can build on existing work on school development plans and provide a bridge between self-development and review activities with external validation and inspection. Education goals and objectives need to be negotiated between the main stake-holders (headteachers, advisers, officers, governors, students, parents and elected members) and then shared with a wider public. Establishing and clarifying the goals and objectives is a central learning process in itself which can help to improve the quality

Measuring Quality

of the educational experience offered to pupils. One group of schools working with advisers in their LEA authority outlined their principles and initial priorities in the following terms.[3]

Principles for the Development of an Education Indicators Framework

- Education indicators must be meaningful to everyone interested in education.
- They should help us compare one school with another.
- They should focus on issues about which we should gather information and on which we can act.
- An individual school/college should be able to measure itself against what it thinks is important, as well as more general indicators.
- Education is about social as well as academic development and indicators must include both.

Part of the process of change is to develop a shared agreement about education goals and the achievement of those goals. One way of achieving this agreement (as John MacBeath suggests in chapter 8), is by using pupil, parent and teacher surveys to establish the consumer view about the quality of teaching and learning. Such a strategy could focus on issues such as:

— *equality of opportunity*: whether race and gender influence the expectations that schools have about their pupils, or the opportunities offered to them;
— *learner involvement*: whether pupils are empowered through the learning process, or face barriers to their learning;
— *individual school ethos*: whether this is reflected in how the pupils experience the different schools;
— *and academic achievement*: how and what schools recognize by achievement and how they reward it.[4]

Education indicators could be developed on three levels:

(i) *Local education authority service indicators* which the LEA could develop in partnership with schools and colleges, to evaluate the effectiveness of the central services which it provides to institutions.

(ii) *LEA-wide institution service indicators* which could be developed in partnership with schools and colleges and would focus on key elements of the services provided by all schools and institutions. These indicators would be subject to external evaluation and have the particular purpose of widening accountability.
(iii) *School-derived indicators* which would reflect the objectives and values of individual schools. The school-derived indicators would be an extension of the school development plan.

The development of such a framework is not without difficulties. Both teachers and advisers have been overwhelmed by the sheer volume of administrative and organizational change brought about by the Education Reform Act 1988 and subsequent legislation. It is unsurprising, therefore, that in some instances the development of education indicators has been seen as another impossible burden imposed by the LEA, rather than an integral part of the process of setting the new education agenda and part of a new partnership between schools and the LEA.

Teachers reeling from the pressures and concerned about the impact of the publication of raw examination results have at times backed off from developing a broader indicators framework. Yet performance on examination results and standard assessment tasks, pupil attendance and postschool destination are the education indicators which are in the public arena and therefore those on which judgments will be made. The challenge to teachers is to contribute to the development of an education indicators framework which will have a broader definition of pupil achievement which will reflect the quality of teaching and learning.

The approach to the development of education indicators outlined in this section could contribute to that broader definition of achievement. It is an approach which:

— focuses on the process of developing indicators with a range of stake-holders;
— draws on self-evaluation by building on school development planning;
— gives validity to internal school judgments by checking these out against agreed external criteria;
— has its roots in accountability and the improvement of academic achievement;
— and recognizes the need to share information with a wider public.

Measuring Quality

Current Dilemmas and Future Issues

The development of an effective education indicators system at school and local authority level poses many dilemmas and challenges. For the future, the major challenge to schools and local authorities will be to link the development of education indicators, to improvements in the quality of the education service. All this will have to be achieved against a backcloth of reduced resources; diminishing powers for LEAs; and major restructuring of local government.

This task is likely to become even more difficult because of the new national requirements for inspection which sever inspection from support for improvement: a development which is likely to lead to discontinuity rather than progression. The work of schools needs to be subjected to external validation, but the gap also needs to be bridged between that validation process and mechanisms to support improvement. Schools will not automatically improve because they have been inspected, no matter how public the findings of those inspection processes are. Test performance will not automatically improve because results are made public.

A danger for the future is that quality will increasingly be equated with performance on government league tables which measure limited competencies, and are only a partial reflection of academic achievement.

For the future a number of other issues remain unresolved about the *audience* and the *usage* of indicators.

— Who constitutes this wider audience — school governors, elected members, parents, the media?
— How will this audience use the information provided?
— Will this information improve choice, if so what about those parents who have little or no choice?
— Should education indicators be used as a basis for allocating or reallocating resources?
— Should schools, or local authorities, be rewarded for example for the achievement of equality goals or penalized for their failure to achieve them?

The message from the ground is that schools and local authorities are striving to improve quality in an increasingly market orientated and alien climate. In the words of one headteacher:

> Frankly, as the headteacher of a school in a small, relatively poor, urban enclave, I despair for the future, as this movement towards the publication of raw data continues apace . . .

Whilst I am confident that the staff, governors and parents of pupils already in the school will be satisfied with the broader indicators of the school's true performance, I fear that prospective parents, especially the more mobile ones, will be unduly influenced by the publication of raw data which will show the school to be performing badly in comparison with its neighbours in the 'leafy suburbs'.

Only time will tell with this dilemma. We will continue to commit ourselves to all our pupils in equal measure for as long as possible; regularly reviewing and evaluating their progress and taking great satisfaction from the evidence of added value which continues to shine through. However, there may come a time when competition for pupils is such that we will have to skew our resources and compromise our ideals.

Appendix I: Stages in the Development of Education Indicators

* PRINCIPLES
  — What are the guiding principles for the development of indicators?
  — What realistic objectives can be set for the development of education indicators?
  — How do education indicators relate to our main education purposes?
  — How will education indicators be used?

* PROCESS
  — How can we ensure that the process for the development of indicators includes all the 'stake-holders'?

* FOCUS
  — What should be our specific focus?
  — How does that focus relate to our specific aims and purposes?

Basic managerial issues must also be resolved:

— Do we have the organizational capacity to deliver the objectives?
— Do we have clarity of purpose?
— Do all the 'stake-holders' understand the purposes and objectives of indicators?

Acknowledgments

This chapter draws on material from a paper by the author produced for the Local Management Board (1992) entitled 'Quality Effectiveness and Evaluation' which was part of a wider project 'Education: A Major Local Authority Service?'

Notes

1. Unfortunately, early exemplifications of this model tended to obscure the impact of services on consumers. National Health Service indicators on bed occupancy rates, for example, failed to distinguish between those patients who had quit their beds because they were well and those who had quit them because they had died: an object lesson in the limitations of indicators.
2. The relationship between these indicators and the new national inspection system is as yet unclear.
3. The author worked for some time with a group of teachers and advisers in one LEA to develop education indicators.
4. For a fuller discussion of these issues, see Riley (1993).

References

CARTER, N. (1989) 'Performance indicators: Backseat driver or hands off control?', *Policy and Politics*, **17**, 2, pp. 131–8.

CARTER, N. (1991) 'Learning to measure performance: The use of indicators in organisations', *Public Administration*, **69**, Spring, pp. 85–101.

DEPARTMENT OF EDUCATION AND SCIENCE (1989a) *School Indicators for Internal Management: An Aide-Mémoire*, London, HMSO.

DEPARTMENT OF EDUCATION AND SCIENCE (1989b) *The Use Made by Local Education Authorities of Public Examination Results* (Report by HMI), London, HMSO.

Education Counts: An Indicator System to Monitor the Nation's Educational Health (1991) Report of the Special Study Panel on Education Indicators to the Acting Commissioner of Education Statistics, July, National Center for Education Statistics.

GRAY, J., JESSON, D. and SIME, N. (1991) 'Developing LEA frameworks for monitoring and evaluation from research on school effectiveness: Problems, progress and possibilities' in RIDDELL, S. and BROWN, S. (Eds) *School Effectiveness Research: The Messages for School Improvement*, Education Department, The Scottish Office. London, Jessica Kingsley.

NUTTALL, D.L. (1991) 'International education indicators: Theoretical aspects', paper presented to the General Assembly of the INES Project International Education Indicators, Lugano, September.

RILEY, K.A. (1990) 'Making indicators consumer friendly', *Education*, 11 May, pp. 470–2.
RILEY, K.A. (1992) *Education Indicators and the Search for Quality*, Luton, Local Government Management Board.
RILEY, K.A. (1994) *Quality and Equality: Promoting Opportunities in Schools*, London, Cassell.

Chapter 8

A Role for Parents, Students and Teachers in School Self-Evaluation and Development Planning

John MacBeath

This chapter describes the development and uses of one approach to self-evaluation in Scottish schools. It describes the part played by parents, pupils, and teachers in the development of the evaluation instruments, how different schools went about the administration and processing of the data, culminating in school development planning.

The Scottish Context — Some History and Background

Scotland, although part of the United Kingdom, has a distinctively different educational system from England, Wales and Northern Ireland. National policy is set by the Scottish Office Education Department (SOED), and there is a National Curriculum Council, a National Examination Board, and a National Educational Research Council who work closely with the SOED. A national body of Her Majesty's Inspectors (HMI) play a monitoring and support role with primary and secondary schools. A newly-created SOED Audit Unit monitors school standards nationally and publishes information for schools, school boards and parents, on the state of the the nation's schools.

The SOED must work closely with the twelve regional authority departments of education who make their own policies within the framework of SOED guidelines. They look after the day-to-day administration of schools, are responsible for school building and closure, hiring and firing of staff, and are powerful bodies with their own advisory and quality assurance teams, and in some cases their own inspectorate. There is, perhaps inevitably, a tension between the national authority and the regional authorities, exacerbated by political control which resides at both the regional and national levels.

A Role for Parents, Students and Teachers

Educational Glasnost

Perhaps one of the most significant shifts at national level in the last few decades has been the move to greater accountability and greater openness, exemplified by the introduction of:

- school boards, with a constitutional parent majority
- staff development and appraisal for all teachers and senior management
- a Parent's Charter (part of a wider Citizen's Charter), including a requirement on schools to publish reports on their performance

As part of this there has been a move, on the one hand, to a strengthening of the national policy-making and monitoring role, and on the other, to a devolution of more responsibility to individual schools through mechanisms such as giving schools more budgetary control, more control over staff appointments, and ultimately more responsibility for their own success or failure. Schools are placed in much more of a market economy in which there is more explicit competition than ever before. By definition, these forces tend to strengthen power at the national level and at the level of the school, weakening the influence of the regional authority.

The Introduction of Indicators

During the last three years the Scottish Office Education Department has placed a high priority on the development of a comprehensive set of indicators at a national level, working closely with regional authorities to foster some ownership on their part, and encourage their commitment to helping schools in turn to assume ownership of these. In other words, it was hoped that school administrators and classroom teachers would not see this as yet another imposition on their time and goodwill, but as something they could influence, and that would be useful to them.

In order to develop a balanced set of indicators small teams were commissioned to work on different aspects of these. One team worked on the development of indicators related to exam performance, another on qualitative indicators, and a third took on indicators of attitudes to school. The third of these is the subject of this chapter.

Measuring Quality

Developing an Approach

In the Scottish context the development of indicators which rest to a large degree on the views of pupils and parents, is seen in some quarters as both threatening and of dubious validity. The historical context is one in which schools and teachers have seen themselves as authorities and as professionals, and parents have to a considerable extent been happy to collude with the notion that education takes place in school at the hands of highly trained practitioners, and that parents support the school by their confidence and trust in the integrity of the professionals. This deference to the professionals was exemplified when school boards were introduced in 1989. A widespread response was to put up for election those parents who stood on a hands-off ticket, promising not to 'interfere' in the professional business of teachers.

What weight can we place on pupil and parent views anyway, it is argued, since pupils have a limited understanding, and parents even more so? Can pupils be counted on to be fair, to take a long view, to take the exercise seriously?

However, it is also often argued that a teacher's, or a school's, most valuable sources of feedback are pupils, fellow teachers and parents. Regrettably they do not often offer such information voluntarily, and systematic evaluation which includes their views is not common practice. When pupils express their appreciation or parents write in to thank a teacher, it is most gratifying. When they offer criticism it is often less easy for teachers to accept because it seems like an isolated attack without context and without acknowledgment of all the effort, and of often inconspicuous work which is all too easily taken for granted.

The task facing the development team, then, was to to create a form of systematic evaluation and feedback which recognized the potential threat and the potential reward, and at the same time acknowledged that any such enterprise would not only be sensitive but be time-consuming and resource-consuming as well. It was agreed at an early stage that the process should be 'owned' by the school itself, and not seen as something imposed from outside (by the Inspectorate or the regional authority).

Given the demands of time, economy, and logistics, the main instrument developed to get at the views of the main players was a set of questionnaires. In order for them to meet the criteria of being economical, user-friendly, and yet with some validity, teachers, parents, and pupils had to be involved in the design. A pilot questionnaire was put together and then trialled with headteachers and groups of teachers, parents, and pupils. For example, pupils in groups of about twenty were asked to fill out a questionnaire individually, then they were split into groups of five to (i) discuss their responses together; and (ii) make suggestions about addition or replacement of items which *they* thought would say something important about their school or their teachers.

On the basis of a series of such trials the questionnaires were revised and revised again. This process brought with it some additions and modifications to the questionnaire approach itself. Such an instrument could not, for example, be used with pupils in the younger years of primary schools, nor with nursery school children, nor could it be used for children with learning difficulties. Alternatives were devised, such as giving to teachers of very young children a discussion schedule which they could use with children in a non-threatening environment (for example, the child sitting on the teacher's knee).

The Questionnaires

The Parent Perspective

The kinds of questions suggested by parents confirmed the findings of many of the studies undertaken on parental priorities. Parents wanted to have answers to question such as:

Is my child:
- enjoying school?
- happy?
- safe?
- well behaved and learning good behaviour?
- able to get on with other pupils?
- being treated fairly by teachers?
- being given the fullest opportunities to learn?
- being helped to make the best choices?

These were then translated into a questionnaire format. Questions from sources other than parents were also incorporated if it was felt by teachers or school management that they would yield useful information but might not have been spontaneously offered by parents themselves. The following is an example of the kind of protocol for parent questions:

Measuring Quality

EXAMPLES OF QUESTIONS TO PARENTS:

	strongly agree	agree	disagree	strongly disagree
'I really feel they know my child as an individual'				
'I know that if my child is having difficulty he/she will be helped'				
'I am happy that my child is being given the fullest opportunities to learn'				
'Sometimes there's too much homework and at other times very little or none'				
'I am confident that if there's a problem they'll let me know immediately'				

The Pupil Perspective

The kinds of questions which pupils wished answers to were, for example:

- If you don't understand something will the teacher help you?
- Does the teacher tell you how you are getting on?
- Can the teacher control the class?
- Can the teacher take a joke?
- Do you get punished for things you didn't do?
- Do teachers apologize when they are in the wrong?
- Do teachers pick on you or treat you all the same?

Again these were translated into a questionnaire format and questions added.

EXAMPLES OF QUESTIONS TO PUPILS:

THINGS THAT MIGHT HAPPEN	would never happen	unlikely to happen	likely to happen	happens often
A teacher made fun of someone in front of the class				
A pupil cracked a joke about the teacher and the teacher took it in good part				
A pupil didn't understand the class work but was too afraid to ask for help				
A teacher went out of her way to encourage and praise pupils who were not very good at classwork				

A Role for Parents, Students and Teachers

The Teacher Perspective

While sharing similar concerns to pupils and parents, teachers saw their ability to teach effectively as dependent on how they themselves were treated, their conditions of service, their morale, and the overall management of the school. Questions they are interested in are, for example:

- Is the school environment pleasant to work in?
- Is there a climate of discipline?
- Do you get the resources you need to do the job?
- Do you get support from management?
- Do you get support from parents?
- Are decisions made with or without consultation?
- Is staff development time used effectively?

EXAMPLES OF QUESTIONS TO TEACHERS:

	strongly agree	agree	disagree	strongly disagree
'I often feel my abilities have not been recognized'				
'I get the feeling that I am listened to and my views are taken seriously by promoted staff'				
'It is difficult to talk to anyone in school about problems in my teaching'				
'I get a lot of help and support from my colleagues'				
'Staff development time is used effectively'				

The Perspective of Headteachers and Senior Management

Headteachers and senior management, while having an interest in all these questions, also wanted to know how they were seen by staff, pupils and parents:

- Is there effective communication? with staff? with parents? with pupils?
- Do staff feel they are involved in decision-making?
- Are different subject departments treated equitably?
- In special schools is the contribution of non-teaching staff recognized and valued?

Measuring Quality

- Is there effective monitoring of teaching?
- Is there effective monitoring of administrative staff?
- How is the headteacher regarded? by staff? by parents? by pupils?

Each different set of players clearly wanted information that was important to them and their role and task, and both evaluation and school development planning need to start from that premise. It needs to take account of both the idiosyncratic and the shared concerns, and acknowledge that an effective school is one that is effective for everybody. All parties have a common interest in a pleasant and productive environment, safety, good discipline, good relationships, motivation and enjoyment in learning, success and achievement.

It was agreed by all those involved that as the main instrument of evaluation, the questionnaires should meet the following criteria:

- be engaging,
- be user friendly,
- be concise,
- use unambiguous terms and language,
- tap a wide range of aspects of school and classroom life,
- gauge common concerns from three or more different viewpoints,
- gauge concerns which are specific to different viewpoints,
- provide space for open-ended comment.

It was also agreed that the questionnaires would contain a number of core questions which would be answered by all 'players', and so allow comparisons (or triangulations), and also questions which were specific to each group's peculiar interests.

The Pilot

The next stage was a full scale pilot study involving a national sample of twenty-three schools — ten secondary, ten primary, one nursery and two special schools. The purpose of this was essentially to test the instrument in a range of different contexts — small and large schools, denominational and non-denominational schools, well-off schools and schools in areas of poverty, schools in the highlands and in the lowlands.

The running of this exercise in twenty-three different schools from consultation to reporting, and ultimately school development planning provided a wealth of experience and models of practice to offer to other schools, which was brought together in a self-evaluation guide for schools, published by the Scottish Office Education Department in summer 1992. It drew together the experience of the schools, providing case studies of how different schools had gone about it and suggesting guidelines for administration, collection and analysis of data, and dissemination.

For example it outlined a number of key principles that had been formulated by schools on the basis of their experience. The following is an extract from that document:

1 People need to know why the survey is being conducted
Teachers like to be consulted and dislike impositions on their time and goodwill. Explanations at staff and departmental meetings and opportunities for discussion in smaller groups is critical. Prior consultation on questions, administration and processing is both judicious and helpful, as there are always new and ingenious ideas. The same is true of school Boards. Opportunities for them to make their own suggestions and contributions is likely to give them a greater insight into, and commitment to, the exercise. The same principle may be applied to pupils, or pupil representative groups.

2 Participants need to know what is going to be done with the information
Knowledge of how the information will be used is particularly significant for teachers. Comments and judgements made by pupils and parents may be critical of them and they have to be reassured that no individuals will be identified in reporting the findings. Teachers are also likely to have to put into effect any action or innovation resulting from the survey. Pupils tend to be more philosophical, accepting it as one of these things that happens in school, but this is not a justification for ignoring their rights and potential educative functions of the exercise for them.

3 Honest and useful statements of opinion depend on the assurance of confidentiality
Ensuring confidentiality is an essential element in obtaining honest and therefore useful answers. But there are also a myriad of ways of beating the system and it is difficult to achieve complete confidentiality. For example, perceptive and knowledgeable teachers can often identify individuals from the information on a particular form. It is, therefore, important that those in charge of the exercise ensure

Measuring Quality

that teachers are carefully briefed about the protocol and the procedures for collecting and storing of the questionnaires, and about respecting pupils' rights not to disclose what they have written.

These may seem obvious principles but were written into the guidelines because they had frequently been observed to be breached. Confidentiality is a good example. There was a lot of discussion as to whether it was necessary. Headteachers, especially in small primary schools, tended to argue that theirs was a friendly and open staff and that there was no need for confidentiality. There were some surprises for those heads even in the apparently cosiest of little schools. In one such five teacher school staff got their husbands to write comments to disguise their handwriting and even choice of vocabulary because that was the only way in which they could honestly express their feelings without perceived recrimination.

The confidentiality principle was equally sacrosanct with pupils, but there were always ways around it, both crude and sneaky. After collecting the questionnaires from his class one teacher was overheard going through the questionnaire item by item, saying

Hands up those who said they enjoyed going to school.

In another school a guidance teacher admitted to the following:

I used the five finger trick. What I do is I spread the fingers of my hand and when the particular forms are handed that I want to be able to identify them later I slide them between my fingers and hold them like that.

This teacher's reasoning was that there were one or two pupils' forms that he wanted to check because these were children at risk and their responses might therefore be important for guidance purposes. This laudable intent has, however, to be set against the promise of confidentiality, and even teachers who had for honourable reasons tried to subvert it, ultimately had to agree that a promise was a promise.

From Guidelines to Practice

The guidelines appeared in 1992 as a fairly substantial volume along with three companion volumes, distinguishable at a distance by their psychedelic dressing. The first volume (bright blue) was on indicators of secondary examination performance,[1] the second and third (orange and bright green) were on qualitative indicators for primary and secondary,[2] the fourth and fifth (bright pink and lilac) were published as 'ethos indicators' because they rested perceptions of rather ethereal school qualities such as the parent-friendliness, morale, relationships, feelings of being safe, cared for, challenged.[3]

A set of twelve 'ethos indicators' was suggested as a framework for collecting and analyzing data. These were offered not as holy writ but as examples of indicators that a school might use for examining its ethos and relationships, and a way of systematizing its self-evaluation and development planning.

The Indicators

The twelve suggested indicators were:

- pupil morale
- teacher morale
- teachers' job satisfaction
- the physical environment
- the learning context
- teacher-pupil relationships
- discipline
- equality and justice
- extra-curricular activities
- school leadership
- information to parents
- parent-teacher consultation

For each of these indicators a short definition was also suggested. For example, for the first-pupil morale — the following definition was offered:

Pupil Morale

The degree to which pupils enjoy school and feel that what they are learning is interesting and relevant.

Under each indicator heading a procedure was suggested as to how to go about collecting data which would offer evidence in that area, again

Measuring Quality

with the encouragement to think creatively about how you could go about such an exercise economically, sensitively, and with validity.

The message from the SOED was that these guidelines were not to be an instrument in the hands of the Inspectorate or local authority, but that a school undertaking this process should embark on it because it believed that it was for its own good, that it would as a result be a better school, or would at least know more clearly what to do in order to become one. The more that evaluation process was a whole school enterprise in which everyone had some investment, the more likely the chance of success.

Ownership was more likely to be enhanced if schools adopted the framework and process and added, subtracted, or modified, questionnaire items to meet their own needs and circumstances, or indeed developed quite different approaches to the gathering of information or 'evidence'.

Development of Alternative Approaches

It is easy, especially for a hard-pressed school, to simply follow a received protocol and to do it ritualistically because it is expected. This clearly has happened in some schools without any sense of ownership or investment in the process. In some cases a school with imagination, initiative and residual energy, has taken it on with enthusiasm and engaged the whole staff in a development exercise that has excited and invigorated everyone.

In some cases schools have needed the push or the support of the local authority to carry out the exercise. One Scottish authority, Central Region, invited interested primaries and secondaries to be part of a network of schools who would together take the ideas further. Participating schools were promised support from advisers and from an outside consultant, and some staff development time, to come up with their own ideas.

In one school a primary 4 teacher involved her class in thinking through how they would evaluate teaching and learning in their own classroom. The pupils gave her some critical feedback on the instruments she had devised and with her encouragement reworked the forms to make them more usable and pupil-friendly.

In another school the headteacher, who had in her two years tenure tried to create a completely different school kind of school ethos, and wanted to know if she had really taken people with her. The school's values (cooperation, care for one another, equality of the sexes, anti-aggression) were, to some extent, antithetical to those of the community. The combination of high unemployment and entrenched chauvinist traditions worked together to create expectations of the school which ran at cross-grain to those of the head and the teachers. The parents had previously been hostile to many of the things the school was trying to do.

The staff wanted to know if pupils had actually internalized those values and ways of behaving which the school was trying to foster. Did pupils really begin to respect each other regardless of ability or sex? Did they really intervene to stop aggression and bullying or to report it to the pupils' behaviour committee? Did they really see the teachers and the headteacher as someone they could go talk to and help resolve their disputes or anxieties?

The school selected two indicators — *discipline* and *the learning context* to explore. By dint of clever questionnaire design and a determination to reach all parents no matter how illiterate or inaccessible they succeeded in getting a 100 per cent return. For pupils a form of questionnaire was designed which offered them a hypothetical classroom and two hypothetical pupils — William and Mary — asking them to say how much like their own classroom, and William and Mary's experience, their experience was.

The success of this impelled the headteacher to push the concept further. With support from the authority, she decided to experiment with a visual formula consisting of a series of snapshots of school and classroom life. These snapshots would be literally *snapshots*, acquired by someone with an automatic camera spending a day in the school and capturing key moments of classroom and school life.

This comprehensive collection (six rolls of film and 218 pictures) was then sifted to find between a dozen and two dozen shots which would be most generative of ideas, and discriminating in the interpretations being offered. For example, one shot from behind the headteacher's desk showed a 7-year-old entering the headteacher's room. The questions 'What is happening here?', 'What is the headteacher saying?', 'What is the pupil saying?', 'What will happen next?' led to a range of responses. The desired answer would be something like 'He is there to show Mrs. Ross the poem he has just written.' Analyzing the range of different answers allowed the school to gauge one item of evidence on the extent to which the headteacher's objectives of a positive supportive school climate had been realized in practice.

Field-testing and validating the individual pictures is work currently

Measuring Quality

in progress, and already there are all kinds of possibilities foreseen for using this formula with parents and with staff whether in an assessment or in a planning and development context.

Dealing with the Data

Whatever the approach used it will generate a considerable body of either quantitative or qualitative data. Given the opportunity pupils will write frankly and perceptively. The following are just a small and quite typical sample of the kinds of things pupils wrote:

> All my classes are good natured. Most of them make school slightly more fun. If teachers would not talk like teachers and treat us like adults, the day would pass quicker and maybe a higher standard of work would be given in at the end of the day.

> This is a very good school but some teachers destroy the pleasantness by being to strict or not having a sense of humer.

> Our maths teacher is unfair he will say 'I don't understand how you can't understand this!' and I feel like saying 'Nor do I!'.

> I agree that some teachers are ok but others are just out to see who they can hurt or make a fool of you.

> I would like school to be a place of happiness, more freedom and trust should be given to most pupils.

Not all children could, of course, express themselves in that medium. Some schools found imaginative alternatives for very young children or for children with writing difficulties. In one school primary 7 youngsters acted as scribes for primary 3. In another school the teacher gave children ten minutes to go off to another room with a tape recorder to record their views. In some schools a learning support teacher took pupils through a schedule of pictures or questionnaire items.

How all of this data can then be analyzed, interpreted and used constructively is another question. The process needs to be economical and accessible for schools who cannot be expected to work out correlations, clusters and standard deviations.

A Role for Parents, Students and Teachers

With the qualitative data the simplest procedure (although time consuming) is to total the number of times a particular issue is mentioned. These are one school's figures:

PUPIL COMMENTS — *summary*

	No. of pupils
run down condition of school	146
lack of facilities	136
desire for uniform	111
unequal treatment	99
litter problem	90
complaints about toilets	86
request for longer lunch hour	79
need for more understanding by teachers	69
praise for teachers	65
teachers jumping dinner queue	58
desire for more extra-curricular activities	56
timetabling issues	55
curricular issues	51
lack of effective discipline	49
comments about good school	47
nowhere to go at breaks	45
returning adults treated better	41
I like PE/more PE	40

This data may then be cross-referenced back to the set of indicators, and to the quantitative data that has also been collected.

For example, if the school were to take the first of the twelve indicators — pupil morale — there is evidence from total numbers of pupils writing about unequal treatment by teachers (ninety-nine) or the need for more understanding by teachers (sixty-nine) as well as from heartfelt individual comments. Pupils typically wrote about things to do with their own happiness, safety, anxieties or problems with teachers. There are also many comments which give important clues to relevant action that could be taken by the school, or by teachers, sometimes with helpful pointers to good practice.

> I like the way the headteacher stops the bullying and if you are scared to go home will drive you home. (12-year-old boy)

> In A the upper school in my opinion are treated like adults. In fifth and sixth years the pupils are allowed a wider scope, and can identify with teachers, who in turn, in my opinion make fifth and sixth years feel more adult by treating them with more respect. (upper secondary girl)

Measuring Quality

These might be cross-referred with questionnaire data, for example from this same school:

	all the time	most of the time	sometimes	never
			percentages	
I enjoy being at school	3	48	46	4
I find school work interesting	2	37	58	4
I get bored in class	3	13	78	6
I am unhappy in class	2	5	50	44
I am worried I can't do the work	2	7	61	30
I feel unsafe in the playground	1	1	24	73

	would never happen	unlikely to happen	likely to happen	happens often
'A gang of older pupils bullied younger ones every day in the playground'	12	56	26	6

The SOED guidelines suggest some ways in which this data might be disaggregated:

	percentages (all/most of the time)					
	Y1	Y2	Y3	Y4	Y5	Y6
I enjoy being at school	63	42	51	49	42	65
I find school work interesting	50	32	41	39	33	58

	percentages (likely/happens often)					
	Y1	Y2	Y3	Y4	Y5	Y6
A gang of older pupils bullied younger ones...	47	36	32	30	22	20

	percentages (sometimes)					
	Y1	Y2	Y3	Y4	Y5	Y6
I feel unsafe in the playground	46	29	21	9	0	0

A Role for Parents, Students and Teachers

Disaggregation by sex/gender is a further illuminating process.

(percentages)

		all the time	most of the time	sometimes	never
I enjoy being at school	boys	2	43	51	5
	girls	4	53	41	2
I find school work interesting	boys	3	28	62	7
	girls	1	45	54	2

Schools found it useful to have comparative figures from other schools in order to determine whether these differences, by year group or by gender, were school-specific, or general, differences. While gender differences tended, in fact, to be common to all schools in this study, this did not preclude any given school treating it as a significant issue for them.

Further disaggregation could also be done by home language (Urdu, Bengali, Cantonese, Shona etc.) and in schools where this was relevant it proved a fruitful trail to explore, particularly on issues such as safety in the playground and bullying.

Comparing the Perspectives

The next step in the process is to set pupils' judgments alongside those of teachers and parents. For example, these are parent and teacher answers to the questions on enjoyment and interest:

Parent — 'My child enjoys being at school'
Teacher — 'Most pupils enjoy being at school'

(percentages)

	strongly agree	agree	disagree	strongly disagree
PARENT	2	78	20	1
TEACHER	7	69	25	0

Measuring Quality

Parent — 'My child finds school work interesting'
Teacher — 'Most pupils find school work interesting'

(percentages)

	strongly agree	agree	disagree	strongly disagree
PARENT	1	75	22	1
TEACHER	3	62	35	0

The comparison of perspectives provides the most illuminating information of all. Compare, for example, the following:

The school has explained to parents what part they can play in their child's education

teachers	77%

The school has explained to me what part I can play in my child's education

parents	53%

and
The school explains its homework policy to parents

teachers	89%

The school has explained its policies on homework to me

parents	47%

These kinds of responses have led schools to look more closely at questions such as:

- How do we try to convey messages to parents?
- How do we know the message has been received?
- How do we know if it has been accepted or understood?
- What does it actually mean for parents in day to day reality?
- What more could the school, or individual teachers, do?

A Role for Parents, Students and Teachers

The following triangulation with regard to homework is highly revealing. There is close agreement by all parties on the *amount* of homework, it is discussed or not by teachers seems much more open to question:

'appropriate amount of homework'   *strongly agree/agree*

pupils	57%
teachers	60%
parents	60%

'teachers talk about homework'   *strongly agree/agree*

pupils	27%
teachers	89%
parents	63%

One school in a highly deprived area of Glasgow asked parents to say whether the questionnaire had been filled out by mother, father, or both. On some of the questions there were some striking differences between mothers and fathers:

Mother and father differences

	% agree/strongly agree or 'yes'	
	mother	father
School facilities are adequate	72	29
Teachers treat all pupils fairly	74	36
The school board seems a useful thing	64	36
School buildings are kept clean	83	57
I'm happy about what my child is learning	90	69
Teachers are approachable and sympathetic	87	69
Most pupils find school work interesting	82	64
Meetings are arranged at a time which suits	72	50
Most pupils enjoy school	79	62
Teachers show respect for pupils	73	57

Measuring Quality

This stimulated some interesting debate among staff and within the School Board about the causes of these divergent opinions. One of the most cogent arguments advanced was that fathers tend only to come to school at times of crisis and bad news. The point was also made that given the more positive response to school by girls as against boys this was likely to be perpetuated through to the next generation. Fathers were also, in that area, likely to have left school at the earliest opportunity and to have retained a dim view of their own school experience.

These sharply discrepant responses do raise an issue about the validity of the parent questionnaire but the point that this is an illuminative and developmental exercise, rather than a scientific inquiry, has to be borne in mind.

From Evaluation to Development Planning

One of the central purposes of the exercise is to create a climate and to inform and support the whole process of development planning. Having collected and analyzed the data all schools have been faced with a range of issues, some minor and some highly significant. In all there were implications for short or long-term action.

In the short term, there were issues to do with playgrounds, buildings, and in particular, toilets. In primary and secondary schools alike the biggest write-in of all was about toilets, of which sometimes a quite sordid picture emerged. Toilets seemed to represent the underlife of schools, a place where many pupils feared to tread and therefore reported 'holding on all day till you get home' rather than face the gauntlet of the lavvies. The toilet issue was confirmed and reiterated in responses to the parental questionnaire. Schools were sometimes able to take immediate action on this issue. In the light of the evidence headteachers were less inclined to marginalize toilets as a trivial matter, and more inclined to see them as an important aspect of school ethos.

The longer term issues were discipline, communication, teacher-pupil relationships, staff development, and the leadership of the headteacher. A common strategy followed by schools was to hold a series of follow-up small group seminars, sometimes purely internally, in some cases inviting the researchers as consultants. The latter process allowed hard things to be said to management without anyone individually or collectively having to stick their neck out, and indeed some important things emerged from such meetings.

A Role for Parents, Students and Teachers

At such meetings, groups of seven or eight teachers, drawn from different departments, discussed and added their interpretation of the questionnaire findings. In order for this not to be simply a venting session against senior management, schools were advised that groups be asked to make some concrete suggestions for development planning, and to take some responsibility for future work in specific areas. Taking their own responsibility for staff development, for example, moved one school from disgruntled consumers of management's offerings to providers and constructive evaluators.

In some schools that process was replicated in the School Board and/or PTA and with pupils. In some it was seen by headteachers as a valuable curriculum opportunity. The process itself included issues about research methodology, perceptions and attitudes, gender issues, data analysis, word processing, report writing and presentation, school ethos, management. There was, for those who seized the opportunity, an opportunity for young people to play an integral and educative role in the whole project from questionnaire design to reporting to parents, to the community, and to the media.

Inter-school Comparisons

Currently the information which schools get back has to be interpreted within the context of that individual school, and individual schools have no normative framework with which to compare themselves unless they do it on a local or collegial basis. If it is desirable or useful to compare schools in the first place, is it something that needs to be taken on at national or local authority level?

There are no national league tables of relationships, ethos, caring or concern. It is not at all beyond the bounds of possibility, however, for a local group of schools to exchange results, or for there to be a bank of responses with which schools could compare themselves. For example, a school might justifiably ask 'If 62 per cent of teachers say that staff development time is used effectively, is that a good or a bad result?'. In absolute terms it is somewhat short of 100, but in relative terms (according to the following responses from ten secondary schools) it is relatively good.

The pilot project, being in possession of results from twenty-three schools could offer this kind of normative information to any individual school. For example this was the good news for Happy Valley High School in comparison with nine other secondaries:

Measuring Quality

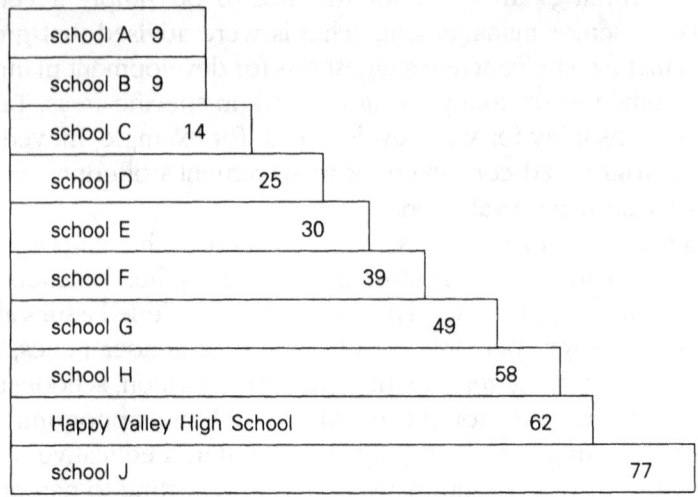

'staff development time is used effectively'
percentages of teachers responding positively

Inter-school comparisons and 'league tables' raise sensitive issues, but if the complaint is that current tables are too narrow and partial then there may be mileage in exploring this idea further. The inclusion of measures of pupil, parent, and teacher perceptions might go some way to filling-out or contextualizing such raw data because it illustrates ways in which low-achieving schools can outperform high-achieving ones in terms of consumer response. There were many examples of this in our twenty-three school study, most strikingly of which were in terms of learning support, guidance, community involvement, teacher-pupil relationships and teacher attitudes. The item 'a teacher swore at a pupil', for instance, proved to be a quite sensitive litmus of teacher attitudes to young people, much more likely to be reported in schools with a 'grammar school' type ethos, rather than in schools in areas of deprivation.

If schools are, in future, to be measured in terms of value-added test/exam achievement we might also want to consider how we might go about evaluating value-added personal, or moral, growth, or even 'value-added ethos'.

Summary

The specificity of the model suggested by the SOED guidelines, whether in content of the questionnaires, the questionnaire items, or the set of indicators should not be regarded as sacrosanct. It provides a model which schools should be free to adapt or radically change. The essential thing is that the process is owned by schools themselves and is part of a whole school development process.

Nor should this approach or set of indicators sit in isolation, but should be complemented by other hard data such as examination performance, attendance rates, take up of extra-curricular activities and so on. The attitudinal data then serves to illuminate and explain some of the bald statistics which never in themselves tell the whole story.

Even then, to quote Kathryn Riley, the indicators should be seen less as barometers than as tin openers, that is not giving us definitive measures of a school's quality but as opening cans of worms. Of course, no school likes cans of worms and will only expose them to the sunlight if there is some faith that they can then be found a less slithery lifestyle.

Notes

1. Using Examination Results in School Self-Evaluation: Relative Rating and National Comparison Factors, SOED, 1991.
2. Using Performance Indicators in Primary School Self-Evaluation, SOED, 1992.
   Using Performance Indicators in Secondary School Self-Evaluation, SOED, 1992.
3. Using Ethos Indicators in Primary School Self-Evaluation: Taking Account of the Views of Pupils, Parents and Teachers, SOED, 1992.

Chapter 9

Measuring Performance — National Contexts and Local Realities

Kathryn A. Riley and Desmond L. Nuttall

Measuring Performance: National Agendas

Over the past decade, the development of measures to assess public sector performance in the United Kingdom has been a growth industry: much influenced by the election of a radical Conservative government in 1979. That government and subsequent Conservative administrations have sought to control public expenditure and assert a new managerialist order based on the three Es of: economy, efficiency and effectiveness.

The rights of individuals, users and consumers of public services have been emphasized through legislation aimed at increasing choice, within and between public services, and through the provision of public information about the quality of those services. In the 1990s, those rights and choices became embedded in the 'Citizen's Charter'.

The government has also sought to regulate the public sector. Thus public services have come under increased scrutiny and the quest for performance indicators to measure the effectiveness of those services has steadily risen. This trend is reflected in the work of the Audit Commission which — in response to the Citizen's Charter — is putting into place a rolling programme of performance indicators for local government aimed at providing information which will enable comparisons to be made between local authorities, on issues of cost, economy, efficiency and effectiveness.[1]

The focus on performance has not been unique to the UK but has been shared by many national governments. National concerns about performance in education have stemmed from the apparent failure of the rapid expansion of education in the 1960s and 1970s, to generate wealth, or to realize social equality. Throughout OECD countries, two simultaneous trends have emerged to tackle the perceived deficiencies in the education system: reforms at the school level and the monitoring of performance from the centre. Where governments have differed is in the strategies they have employed to measure performance and in their views about accountability.

The Education Agenda

In the UK political scepticism about the quality of the education service had begun to emerge in the 1970s and became a feature of legislation in the late 1980s. Central government set out to challenge professional and producer control in education and in other public services. Accountability for performance was to be shifted from the educational professionals and local authorities, to central government and to consumers.

Market mechanisms were put into place through the introduction of new types of schools (grant-maintained and city technology); increased competition between schools; and through the introduction of new competitive inspection procedures. Contracts and charters were also introduced into the public service as mechanisms to improve quality and further the rights of individual citizens.

The UK government's views about quality in education have been asserted through the introduction of the National Curriculum and attainment targets. Pupil outcomes are to be judged through the publication of school performance on public examinations and on nationally set tests with attainment targets based on notions of hierarchies of skills and tasks. A new semi-privatized four-yearly inspection system has been established to report on individual school performance and identify failing schools. An underlying assumption behind these changes was that those products (schools) which failed the consumer test would go out of business.

Although the role of local authorities in assessment, monitoring and evaluation has been diminished, the impact and application of educational changes throughout the UK has not, however, been uniform — a point illustrated in chapter 7. Both Northern Ireland and Scotland have resisted, or been exempt from, elements of the national prescription. The absence to date of any grant-maintained schools in Scotland has reduced the competitive framework. Scotland has also developed a less rigid approach to testing, largely in response to parental and professional objections. The extent to which the 1993 teachers' boycott of national testing in England and Wales will act as a long-term counterweight to central government prescription remains to be seen.

International Comparisons

Although governments share a concern for national goal setting; for information about educational outcomes; and for monitoring they have responded to issues about performance and outcomes in different ways. UK governments since 1979 have sought to achieve quality through the development of a new evaluative system, a process which has been described as 'The Rise of the Evaluative State': the growth in evaluative instruments (for institutions or authorities) which serve as indirect forms of control — ways of checking whether centrally determined objectives have been achieved (Carter, 1991). As part of this shift, the UK has witnessed a move away from professional accountability for performance — previously based on self-evaluation and peer review — to more public forms of accountability, based on other forms of evaluation such as external inspection, or performance indicators.

The UK framework has been more heavily prescribed and market orientated than other European and OECD countries. It also reflects a significant shift in power from local government to central government: a trend which runs counter to power shifts in many other countries. Hungary, for example, has shifted educational responsibilities from central government to both regional government and to local school areas (Petrikas, 1992). Norway is moving towards a more decentralized system and through its 'free kommun' initiative is experimenting with ways of reducing central government controls on local authorities. Sweden has also decentralized significant education powers to school districts and developed an approach to evaluation and the improvement of quality which is a strikingly different way to the UK.

An Alternative Approach to Evaluation: Sweden

The Swedish government has set up the National Agency on Education (NAE) to establish a comprehensive national assessment programme to calibrate the education system. The national assessment programme has been designed firstly, to provide information to central government about the achievement of national goals and priorities and secondly, to provide information to the kommuns (local authorities), so that they can stimulate schools and support school improvement. Over two-thirds of the staff of the National Agency on Education are involved in reviewing the efforts of the 284 Swedish kommuns on education, as a way of improving the school system.

NAE has used a broad range of instruments to assess both cognitive outcomes (performance in grade tests) and non-cognitive outcomes. The NAE analysis of schooling has drawn on both quantitative and qualitative material, performance data, background data, process data, observations and longitudinal studies.

In 1992, NAE set up an evaluative project to examine pupils' non-cognitive development. The emphasis on non-cognitive outcomes has served to broaden the debate about the processes and goals of schooling. The project (which looked at 10 per cent of Swedish schools) took as one of its major sources of information the views of pupils themselves who were judged to be 'connoisseurs of their own schools'. It examined pupil's development on four core variables which reflected strong national purposes: *independence, self-confidence, participation in decision-making* and *solidarity with others*.

The attempt to assess how far individuals had a critical mind and were able to act independently stemmed from a view that:

> Individuals that hold a critical mind and are used to act in independent ways are seen as important parts of the 'assurances' that the Swedish society have taken towards fascism.
> (Ekholm and Karang, 1993, p. 13)

Self-confidence was seen as a prerequisite for successful learning, and involvement in decision-making, as essential to sustaining democracy. Tolerance and understanding of others were also seen as essential to democracy.

> Democracy in Sweden is also based on solidarity with other people than the closest ones and on tolerance towards variation among people.
> (*ibid.*, p. 14)

The Swedish national evaluation system has been developed to enable local interpretation and action within a nationally set framework. It is a system which clarifies the respective roles of both central and local government: national government requires information about performance; sets the framework; provides effective information to local authorities; and calls the local system to account for performance. The decentralization of essential aspects of the quality role to local authorities is based on the assumption that the change process required to ensure school improvement is best sustained by a local education system: an assumption at variance with government thinking in the UK.

Measuring Quality

The Swedish example demonstrates how national evaluative systems can be influenced by different national purposes and how information collected about performance can be used in different ways. The critical issue for school improvement is what is the most effective way of using such information? How can schools be moved on?

How to Get Schools Moving

The contributions in this book have focussed both on the context for measuring performance and the application of performance indicators, at both national and systems levels, and at the school level. At a one day workshop on 'Policy Implementation and Practice' held during the International Congress on School Effectiveness (ICSE) Sweden, 1993, practitioners and academics from the UK, Sweden, Holland, the USA and Canada grappled with a number of issues covered by contributors to this book, in particular, the national context for evaluation and the local systems needed to support effective schools.[2] The workshop enabled both the presenters of papers and other participants to examine comparative perspectives on those issues.

Throughout the day, questions raised by the individual contributors coalesced around three themes:

- What is the role of the local authority (or equivalent) in supporting and ensuring school improvement and change?

- What are the most effective mechanisms to support change?
    — inspection?
    — performance indicators?
    — school-based review?
    — accreditation?
    — in-service training?
    — research?

- What makes a local authority effective in supporting school improvement?

A common pattern of thinking emerged — shared not only by the main contributors to the workshop but also by other participants — about the basis for school improvement. Underpinning this thinking was a view that school improvement would not occur, if schools were left to take action on their own.

This analysis was sustained by the experience of school improvement in a range of countries. The Swedish experience indicated that without the combination of external validation and local support, schools would continue to do what they had done in the past. Developments in the USA suggested that schools could not initiate and sustain innovation on their own. Indeed, there was evidence that school-initiated innovation in the States had often been of poor quality and of high cost. UK and Dutch experience suggested that the agenda for action adopted by schools themselves had all too often been based on inadequate data; had rarely been disaggregated on issues of race or gender; and had seldom progressed beyond generalities. Schools needed to be drawn from their isolation and begin to look outwards, if improvement was to be made.

In a piece of work aimed at examining how local systems could contribute to this wider thinking, Canadian researchers Linda Rossler and Larry Sackney drew on a study of twenty-seven school districts in Saskatchewan, to examine what school district practices and norms contributed to effective classroom practices (Rossler and Sackney, 1993). Indicators of effectiveness included a low rate of student drop out, teacher turnover and absenteeism; lack of conflict within the school board; a high incidence of student attendance; school board support, community acceptance; and teacher satisfaction.

The researchers concluded that officers and administrators had a definite influence upon the climate of the school and the classroom and that information provided by the school districts was critical to school improvement. The school district could move on a school that was 'stuck' (one that was not failing but was unable to change and improve) by open, positive communication; collaborative working with schools; and high expectations about performance.

Contributors and participants to the ICSE workshop suggested that there were four elements to the activities required to sustain and support *the learning school*: a school that was equipped to make changes (see figure 9.1).

The first element was the development of *a creative tension between the schools themselves and the communities they served*. Information between parents and schools was critical, if this creative tension was to be sustained. But this information had to be a shared dialogue — as John MacBeath described in his chapter (8) — rather than a one-way exercise, from schools to parents.

A second element was that schools needed to *develop a clear sense of direction*. Again this was something schools could not do in isolation but needed support from their local kommun, school district or local

Measuring Quality

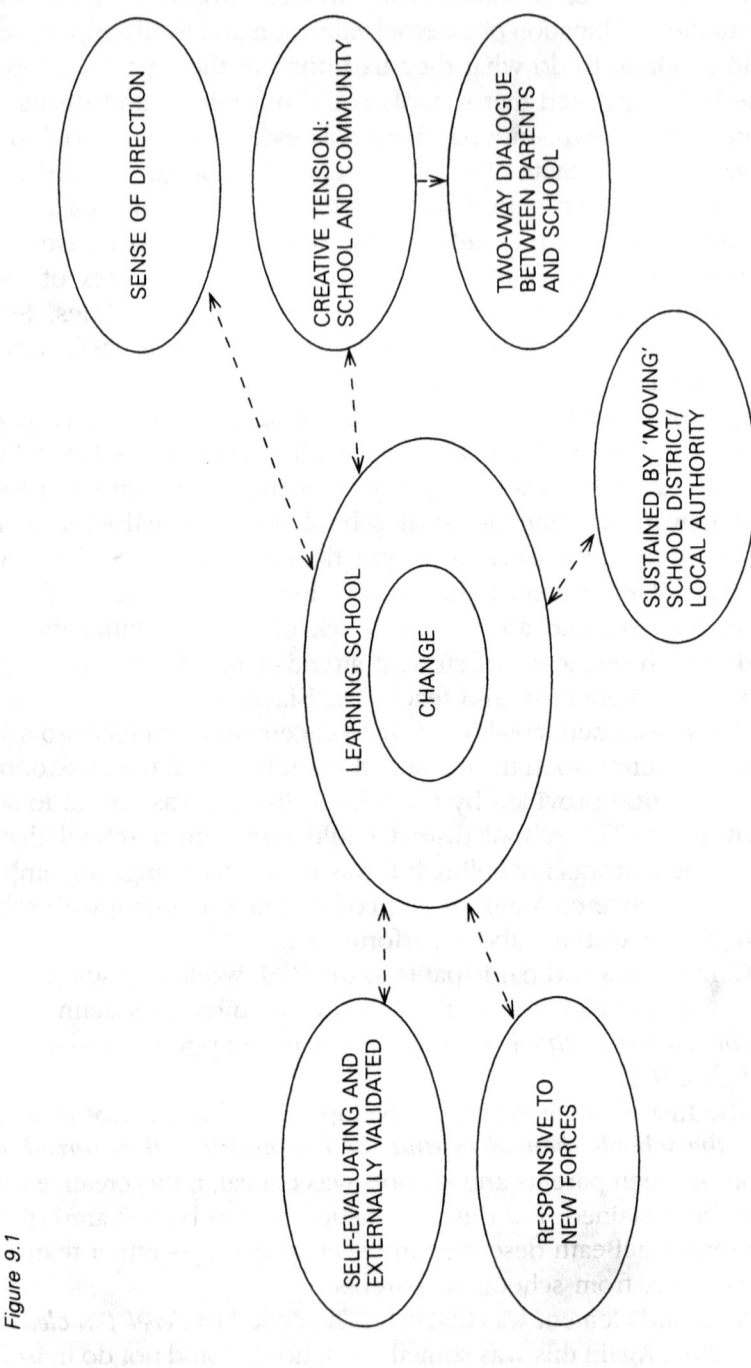

Figure 9.1

authority. Linked to this was a third element. If change was to take place, *schools had be able to absorb and respond to the messages from a complex range of external forces.* The local system could act as a bridge between these external forces and the activities within the schools themselves, matching local needs and interests to national goals or objectives and working with schools to support and embed the change process.

The final element in the activities needed to sustain the learning school was *evaluation — both internal and external.* Evaluation could take place through a range of mechanisms — performance indicators, inspection, or accreditation — and could provide the critical information needed to energise the improvement process within schools and to enable them to find a sense of direction. Information from the local system needed to be provided in two ways: as an instrumental tool to provide direct information and to influence policy decisions and as a conceptual tool, to influence the climate of opinion (Coleman and LaRocque, 1990). For improvement to take place, however, the school's own agenda had to match up to the external agenda: a link had to be created between self-evaluation and external validation.

Local Realities

The ICSE workshop served to highlight the relationship between evaluative systems and school effectiveness. Evaluative systems have the capacity not only to provide information about performance but also to energise and sustain school improvement. International experience suggests that it is difficult for schools to change on their own: their isolation needs to be bridged by a local system, if improvement is to take place. It also suggests that within an evaluative framework which combines self-evaluation with external validation, performance indicators can make their contribution to school improvement. For this to happen, performance indicators need to take into account both cognitive and non-cognitive aspects of learning and reflect the quality of the education experience. Parents, teachers and pupils can be 'connoisseurs of their own schools': an issue on which this book has focussed.

Such an analysis raises questions about the nature and structure of the education system being developed in the UK and whether the values that underpin education should be nationally, or locally determined.

- Is the determination of quality only the business of national government, or should local government have its say?

- Should control and accountability be exercised entirely by central government, or by central and local government and schools?

The 1993 Education Act also raises further critical issues for resolution.

- Who will support schools — both local authority and grant-maintained
  — in a systematic programme of improvement following inspection?
- What will be the most effective system to support schools in a systematic programme of improvement?
- Will the Funding Agency for Schools (FAS) provide such a system, on its own, or in collaboration with local authorities?

Such issues will need to be resolved. In the interim, education indicators can play their role in evaluation and in sustaining school improvement.

Notes

1 The first tranche of the Audit Commission programme (completed in 1994), includes some seventy-seven 'citizen-based' questions about local authorities which are linked to performance indicators. Nine of these questions focus on cost and efficiency issues about the provision of local authority education services and include such questions as: 'how much does it cost to educate the under 5s?'

2 Main contributors to the workshop were:

Canada
Bill McKerlich (Superintendent of Schools, Shuswap, British Columbia), **Linda Rossler** (Assistant Superintendent of Schools, Flin Flon, Manitoba) and **Larry Sackney** (University of Saskatchewan).

Sweden
Mats Exkolm, Rolf Lander (University of Goteborg) and **Oscar Oquist** (National Agency on Education).

UK
John MacBeath (Jordanhill College, Glasgow), **Desmond Nuttall**, Chair of Session (University of London Institute of Education), **Kathryn Riley** (Institute of Local Government Studies, University of Birmingham).

References

CARTER, N. (1991) 'Learning to measure performance: The use of indicators in organisations', *Public Administration*, **69**, spring, pp. 85–101.

COLEMAN, P. and LaROCQUE, L. (1990) *Struggling to be Good Enough: Administrative Practices and School District Ethos,* London, Falmer Press.

EKHOLM, M. and KARANG, G. (1993) 'School-based evaluation as part of a national programme of evaluation: Early results', paper presented to the International Congress for School Effectiveness and Improvement (ICSE), 3–6 January, Norrkoping, Sweden.

ROSSLER, L. and SACKNEY, L. (1993) 'Examining school division effectiveness', paper presented to the International Congress for School Effectiveness and Improvement (ICSE), 3–6 January, Norrkoping, Sweden.

PETRIKAS, A. (1992) *Efficiency of Regional and Local Systems of Education in Hungary*. Paper to the European Conference on Educational Research, University of Twente, Holland, June.

Notes on Contributors

John Gray is Professor of Education at Cambridge University. He co-directs the 'Programme to Assess the Quality of Schooling' (PAQS) with Brian Wilcox which is an ESRC-funded project. He has worked extensively with local education authorities over the last five years to help them establish better frameworks for judging schools' effectiveness using both quantitative and qualitative methodologies.

John MacBeath is Professor and Director of the Quality in Education Centre, Jordanhill College, Glasgow. He has researched and published widely on areas including: school effectiveness and improvement; the role of school boards; and collaborative work across professional divides. He has been a member of the OECD network on Education Indicators which is working to develop indicators around attitudes to, and expectations of, the educational system.

The late Desmond Nuttall until his untimely death, was Professor of Curriculum and Assessment Studies at the University of London, the Institute of Education. He had published widely, particularly in the areas of assessment and evaluation and was co-Director of the 'Differential Schools Effectiveness Project' (ESRC) and Director of the 'Evaluation of Accreditation of Prior Learning Project' (Department of Employment).

Kathryn Riley is Professor and Director of the Centre for Educational Management at the Roehampton Institute, London. She has wide-ranging experience in education and local government and has worked extensively with senior managers in schools and local authorities on education and management issues. Her current research interests are quality, performance and leadership in education and she is co-director — with Kieron Walsh — of the 'The New Management: Citizenship and Institutional Change in Local Governance' (ESRC).

Alan Ruby is the First Assistant Secretary, heading the Schools and Curriculum Division of the Commonwealth Department of Employment, Education and Training, Australia. He has been a consultant to the OECD Centre for Educational Research and Innovation Project on Educational Indicators and has written extensively on this subject. He is currently involved in collaborative work with the United States through his participation in the US-Australia Education Policy Project and is working on the Mayer Committee which is examining the employment-related key competencies concept in education.

Ramsay Selden is Director of the State Education Assessment Centre at the Council of Chief State School Officers, Washington D.C. which leads efforts by States to enhance the breadth, quality and comparability of information about education and to improve the use of that information by educators, educational policy-makers, and the public. Dr. Selden worked at the National Institute of Education prior to joining the Council and has also worked in several capacities with state and local school districts on programme evaluations, student assessments and programme development.

Kieron Walsh is Professor of Public Sector Management, at the Institute of Local Government Studies, University of Birmingham and is the author of a number of books on local government and public sector marketing. His publications include 'Competition for local Authority services' (HMSO, 1991) and 'Marketing and Local Government' (Longman, 1989). His main research interests are the study of public service quality and the development of competition and markets in public service management. He is Director of an ESRC project on contracts and co-director, with Kathryn Riley, of an ESRC project on the new management.

Brian Wilcox is Professorial Research Fellow in the QQSE Research Groups at the University of Sheffield and co-directs the ESRC-funded PAQS Project with John Gray. He was formerly Chief Adviser to Sheffield LEA. His main research interest is the practice of evaluation in education, training and public services.

Index

A Nation at Risk (US) 41–2, 47
ability 10
absolute measurment 57–9
academic progress 33, 36, 81, 93, 97
access
  to indicators 32
  to information 9, 14
  to, knowledge 83
accountability 1, 6, 8, 19, 42–4, 47–8, 49–50, 53, 69, 79–80, 88, 90, 93, 95, 101, 123–4, 130
accreditation 129
accuracy of information 34–5, 42, 45, 49, 53, 65, 89
achievement 10, 14, 28, 30, 41–6, 48, 59, 69, 74, 83, 91, 94–6, 120
adaptation of information 65–6
Aitkin, M. 75
alienation 31
ambiguity of information 60, 62–3, 106
analysis, policy 19–21, 45
Annual National Report on Schooling (Australia) 9
aptitude 42, 45
assessment
  indicators and 36
  of school 32–3
  of services 49, 61
  of student 14, 42, 45–8, 52, 59, 69–70, 72, 74–5, 81–2, 88, 90, 93, 95, 109, 120–1, 123

attendance rates 12–13, 43, 46, 72, 74, 82, 88, 90, 95, 121, 127
audience for information 13–14, 36, 96
Audit Commission 58, 64, 69, 76–7, 122
Australia 8–9, 14–15

Beare, H. *et al* 80
Bibby, J.M. 29
boards, school 101–2, 107, 119, 127
Brennan, R.L. 28
Broadfoot, P.M. 20
budgeting 8, 101
Bulmer, M. 21, 25

Campbell, J. 65
Canada 127
career ladders 8
Carley, M. 20, 25, 34, 35
Carter, N. 51, 57, 87, 89, 124
centralization 8, 10, 124, 130
  de- 45–6, 125
choice 1, 8, 10, 44, 49, 52–3, 96, 122
  of indicators 17–38
Citizen's Charter 49, 53, 64, 66, 101, 122
citizenship 52–3
Civil Service 51
client oriented information 6
Clift, P.S. *et al* 72
Coleman, P. 79, 129

commitment 8, 13, 79–80, 84, 101, 107
communication 118
community, sense of 127–8
comparability
  of indicators 18–19, 22, 31–3, 36, 42, 45–6, 74, 83, 92, 94, 97, 106, 115–17, 122
  of information 6, 9–11, 119–20
  of services 54–6
competition 8, 32, 52, 58, 97, 123
composite indicators 29
comprehensibility
  of indicators 19–20, 30–1, 34–7
  of information 9–11, 14–15
Condition of Education, The (US) 9, 14, 41
confidentiality 107–8
contextualization of information 43, 72–5, 120
control, managerial 51–2, 57, 62, 64–5
controllability of information 9, 32, 35–6
Coopers and Lybrand 69
cost 12, 24–5, 28, 30, 34–8, 52–4, 60, 89, 102, 110, 122
credence good 62
credibility of information 76, 78, 81, 84
Crenson, M.A. 25
Crissey, B.L. 25
criteria for judgment 60–1, 71–2, 75–8, 80, 83, 88, 90
Culyer, N. 61

data collection 10–12, 14–15, 42, 45–6, 54, 90, 109, 110–12, 125
Deaton, A. 54
decision making 1, 7–8, 15, 45, 53, 64, 90, 125
democracy 56, 125
descriptive statements 70–1, 77, 81
desegregation 44

destination, post-16 70, 72, 74, 82, 88, 90, 95
development
  of indicators 31–7, 41, 49, 57, 69, 79, 81, 89–96, 101–2
  planning 100–21
diagnosis, indicators and 31, 45
Dingwall, R. 60
direction, sense of 127–9
directness of information 9
disability 14
discipline 118
dispersion 56
documentation 8

econometric models 21, 25, 29, 37
economy 122
Education Act (1993) (UK) 87, 130
Education Reform Act (1988) (UK) 69, 75, 90, 95
Education (Schools) Act (1991) (UK) 87–8
educational indicators 1, 87–97
effectiveness 8, 122
  of school 1, 28, 33, 69–71, 75–7, 79, 82, 84, 87, 89, 91, 94, 96, 105–6, 126–7, 129
  of services 49, 54–7, 60, 66
efficiency 10, 49, 54, 56, 60, 63, 79, 87, 122
Ekholm, M. 125
empowerment 94
ephemerality of information 12–13
equality 94
ethics 56, 63
ethos 32, 61, 94, 127
  indicators 109–10, 118, 120–1
evaluation
  indicators and 19, 23, 28, 31–7
  of schools 70, 75–7, 79, 81, 88, 89, 93, 95, 97, 123, 126
  self-, of schools 72, 90–2, 95, 100–21, 124, 128–9
  of services 51
exclusion, student 55, 90

Index

expenditure 8, 10, 35, 122
experimentation 56, 62
externalities 54–5

feasibility of indicators 11, 24, 36–7, 53
feedback 35, 57, 102
Feldt, L.S. 28
Fenn, P. 60
Fitz-Gibbon, C.T. 82
Flynn, R. 51
Fox, A. 65
framework, indicator system in 25–6, 28, 30, 36–8
France 13
Fulton Commission 50
Funding Agency for Schools 130

gender 115
generalization 12
goal setting 8, 23, 32, 34, 45–6, 55–6, 69, 79, 89, 91–3, 95, 124–5, 129
graduation rates 43
Gray, John 3, 32, 33, 69–84, 93
Greenberger, M. 25
Griffiths Report 51
Gross Educational Product 29
Gunn, L.A. 20, 23

Hacking, I. 66
Hall, G. 14
Hargreaves, D.H. *et al* 23, 80
Hatry, H.P. *et al* 35
Hau Chow 23–4
headteacher, role of 105–6, 108, 118
Hedger, K. 75
Henkel, M. 64
Hirschman, A.O. 61
Hogwood, B.W. 20, 23
home language 115
homework 116–17
Hoover, H.D. 29
Hopkins, D. 80
Hungary 124

Icarus paradox 59–60
incentives 44–5, 50–2, 57–9, 61, 96
independence 125
indicators, definition of 17–19
INES Project 12, 26, 28, 31
information
   demand for 2, 6–16, 52–3, 61, 122, 126
   indicator 17–19, 22–4
   technology 30
Innes, J.E. 20, 21
inspection of schools 10, 29, 64, 71, 77–8, 83–4, 87, 90–3, 96, 100, 123–4, 129–30
interaction effects 54–5, 61
interpretation of information 15, 18, 21, 30, 56–8, 82, 112–15, 119, 125

Jaegar, R.M. 18–19
Jesson, D. 32, 33, 81, 82
Johnstone, J.N. 17, 18

Karang, G. 125
Kenney, R. 60
Kent, J.T. 29
Kingdon, J.W. 20
Klein, B. 60
Kolen, M.J. 29
Kotler, P. 54

LaRocque, L. 79, 129
leaving school rates 42, 46, 127
level of study 31–2, 34, 36, 38, 43–5
Lightfoot, S.L. 79
limitation
   of information 15
   of measurement 1, 3, 53–7
   of number of indicators 23, 30, 33–4, 36–8, 45, 80, 83, 89
local education authority (LEA) 3–4, 100–1, 123, 126–30
   and use of performance indicators 69–84
Longford, N. 75

MacBeath, John 4, 94, 100–21, 127
McDonnell, L.M. 20, 24
McEwan, N. 23–4
MacRae, D., Jr 21, 30
management 8
    of schools 6, 51, 69–71, 78–9, 90, 93, 118–19
    of services 50–2, 62, 64, 66
manipulation of information 11, 30–1, 45, 54, 63
Mardia, K.V. 29
market mechanism 49, 51–4, 60–1, 65, 96, 101, 123–4
Messick, S. 28
Miller, D. 59
Mitchell, D.E. 7
modelling approach 24–6, 31, 43
monitoring 8, 15, 46, 69, 72, 75, 79, 84, 89, 93, 100–1, 122–4
Mortimore, P. *et al* 61
motivation for information 7–8
Muellbaker, B. 54
Murnane, R.J. 81

National Agency on Education (NAE) (Sweden) 124, 125
National Assessment of Educational Progress (NAEP) 42, 43, 47
national contexts and performance indicators 2–3, 122–30
National Curriculum 52, 56, 81, 83, 123
National Health Service 51, 64
Nelson, P. 61
Netherlands 127
Nisbet, J. 20
Normann, R. 55
Norway 124
Nove, A. 62–3
Nuttall, Desmond L. 2, 4, 17–38, 75, 89, 122–30

Oakes, J. 11, 29, 82, 83
objectivity 69, 76, 88
Odden, A. 30

OECD Indicators Project 25
officials and information 6–16
Osborne, D.A. 23
outcome measures 6, 8, 10, 20, 25–6, 32, 35, 37–8, 45, 58, 61, 74, 81–2, 88–9, 92, 123–5
ownership, sense of 32, 91, 101–2, 110, 121

Parent's Charter 101
parents, role in school self-evaluation 100–21, 123, 127–9
Peters, T.J. 59, 80
Petersen, N.S. 29
Petrikas, A. 124
pluralism 31–2, 92–3
policy analysis and review (PAR) 50
policy context, indicators in 19–26, 30–1, 35–8, 89
policy-planned-budgetting-systems (PPBS) 50
politicization 12, 20, 31, 37
Pollitt, C. 31
Posnett, J. 61
power shift 49, 51, 66, 93, 124
practical issues 30, 37, 89
presentation of information 15, 30
Preston, A.M. 63
problem oriented information 35
process indicators 82, 84
professionalism 56, 102
Programmes to Assess the Quality of Schooling (PAQS) 72
propinquity 12
public services 49–66, 87, 122–3
publication of results 1, 72–4, 83, 88, 95–7, 100–1, 120, 123
pupil
    development 125
    role in school self-evaluation 100–21, 129
    satisfaction 33–4, 81
    teacher ratio 6–7, 29, 34, 43, 70, 81, 118

Index

purpose
  of indicators 17, 19, 37, 53–4, 56, 91–2, 107, 126
  of information 13–14
  of measurement 57–65

quality
  of education 20, 71, 76, 78–9, 81–4, 109, 112–13, 122, 129
  education indicators and 87–97
  of public services 49–66, 122–4
quantifiable indicators 17–19, 34, 51, 70–3, 76, 81, 84, 112–13, 125
questionnaires, use of 102–19

rating scales 77–8, 83–4
realism 57
redundancy of information 23, 34–6
reform, educational 7–9, 41–2, 44, 47, 122–3
relevance of information 12–13, 22, 26, 30, 34, 36–8
reliability of information 14–15, 28–9, 31, 35–7, 110
report cards 43–4
research
  educational 25, 75, 77, 82–4
  knowledge 20, 37
resources 8–9, 96
responsibility 8, 13, 50–1, 61, 101, 124
responsiveness 60, 62, 128–9
rights 122–3
Riley, Kathryn A. 4, 31, 32, 87–97, 121, 122–30
Rockwell, R.C. 20, 35
Rose, R. 20
Ross, S. 61
Rossler, L. 127
Ruby, Alan 2, 6–16
Rumbold, A. 70, 71

Sackney, L. 127
Salganik, L.H. 22

sampling 30
Scheerens, J. 29, 81
school
  improvement strategies 1, 8, 45, 47, 88, 91, 93, 124–7, 129–30
  performance indicators in 69–84
  role 6
School Indicators for Internal Management 88
Scotland, school self-evaluation and development planning in 100–21, 123
Selden, Ramsay 2, 3, 19, 41–8
self-confidence 125
Shavelson, R.J. *et al* 18, 26, 27, 35
Shaw, George Bernard 48
Sime, N. 82
simplicity of information 6, 9, 23, 29
size of class 35
social indicators 20–1, 24–5, 30, 37, 41
social science 18, 21, 29
socioeconomic background 10, 42, 45, 71, 73, 75
specification 15, 26, 28, 52, 60, 71, 76, 84, 106, 120
standardised assessment tests 1, 22, 52, 95, 123
standardization 43, 45–7, 55–6, 69
statistics, use of 18, 29, 42–3, 45, 48, 54, 66, 75
Stern, J.D. 14
subjectivity 29
surveillance 64–5
Sweden 124–6, 127
system
  data 15, 73
  indicator 19–21, 23–4, 29–31, 35, 37–8, 42–3, 79–80, 84, 90, 93, 96
  information 62–3, 65–6

teacher
  characteristics 35, 41
  definition of 7

development 101, 118–19, 120
  role in school self-evaluation 100–21
  tests 8
  training 43, 47
  turnover 127
teaching
  good 77, 83, 94–5, 105
  to test 14, 23, 48
technical issues 26–9, 37, 57, 89
thematic approach 22–3
timeliness of information 6, 9, 30, 34–8, 61–2, 89
toilets 118
tolerance 125
trends 11, 41–2, 71
trust 63–5

United States 8–10, 14, 20, 22, 30, 34–5, 60, 79–80, 87–8, 127
  use of indicators in 41–8
user friendly questionnaires 102, 106

validation, external 92–3, 96, 127–9
validity of information 11, 28–31, 34–8, 42, 45, 95, 102, 110, 118
value added information 10, 23–4, 75, 83, 92–3, 97, 120
value judgments 19–20, 26, 28–30, 54–5, 65, 81, 84, 89–90, 107, 115
van Herpen, M. 20, 25
variables 12, 24–6, 37, 80

Wainer, H. 22
Wallchart (US) 9, 22, 42
Walsh, Kieron 3, 49–66
Waterman, R.H. 59
Weiss, C.H. 20
Wilcox, Brian 3, 69–84, 93
Williams, B. 54
Wilson, J.A. 60
Windham, D. 34

For Product Safety Concerns and Information please contact our EU
representative GPSR@taylorandfrancis.com
Taylor & Francis Verlag GmbH, Kaufingerstraße 24, 80331 München, Germany

www.ingramcontent.com/pod-product-compliance
Lightning Source LLC
Chambersburg PA
CBHW071510150426
43191CB00009B/1471